THE WORLD'S WORST SAILOR
STILL ALIVE TO TELL THE TALE

STEPHEN D. (DOC) REGAN

outskirts
press

The World's Worst Sailor
Still Alive to Tell the Tale
All Rights Reserved.
Copyright © 2022 Stephen D. (Doc) Regan
v2.0

The opinions expressed in this manuscript are solely the opinions of the author and do not represent the opinions or thoughts of the publisher. The author has represented and warranted full ownership and/or legal right to publish all the materials in this book.

This book may not be reproduced, transmitted, or stored in whole or in part by any means, including graphic, electronic, or mechanical without the express written consent of the publisher except in the case of brief quotations embodied in critical articles and reviews.

Outskirts Press, Inc.
http://www.outskirtspress.com

ISBN: 978-1-9772-5839-7

Cover Photo © 2022 Stephen D. (Doc) Regan. All rights reserved - used with permission.

Outskirts Press and the "OP" logo are trademarks belonging to Outskirts Press, Inc.

PRINTED IN THE UNITED STATES OF AMERICA

Dedicated to the women of my life:

Marianne Regan, Jennifer Regan Hale,
Christina Swenson Regan,
Grey Regan, and Briar Regan

Table of Contents

ONE: A KID'S GARDEN OF BOAT BUILDING — 1

TWO: DRIFTLESS ZONE — 5

THREE: FEATS — 9

FOUR: I GOT DA BLUES — 15

FIVE: MY FIRST YEAR SAILING — 20

SIX: MONEY — 30

SEVEN: ROPE: A FIRST YEAR SAILOR'S BEST FRIEND — 35

EIGHT: GODS OF WIND AND SEA — 39

NINE: THE MAGIC OF SAILING — 44

TEN: POKE ABOUT — 49

ELEVEN: MY WIFE HATES SAILING, THANK GOD — 57

TWELVE: NAUTICAL GRIEF	60
THIRTEEN: EXPERIENTIAL LEARNING	62
FOURTEEN: GODS OF THE SEA AND WATER	67
FIFTEEN: I LOVE SMALL BOATS	72
SIXTEEN: POLYSYLLABIC OBNUBILATE VERBIAGE	80
SEVENTEEN: KENNEBUNKPORT AND OTHER RARE DISEASES	83
EIGHTEEN: JET SKIS AS WATER FOWL	88
NINETEEN: USS MARGARET	92
TWENTY: ANXIOUS, DEPRESSED, OBSESSIVE-COMPULSIVE SAILOR IN THE WINTER	97
TWENTY-ONE: FLORIDA RUMINATION	101
TWENTY-TWO: SOME THINGS THAT REALLY P@#%&* ME OFF	106
TWENTY-THREE: NAUTICAL TERMS	111
TWENTY-FOUR: NAUTICAL IQ EXAMINATION	114
TWENTY-FIVE: PATRON SAINTS OF WIND, WATER, AND SAILORS	118
TWENTY-SIX: IOWA WINTER	123
TWENTY-SEVEN: KNIVES	128
TWENTY-EIGHT: BOAT DOGS	132

TWENTY-NINE: SPRINGTIME FOR STUPID STEVE   139

THIRTY: GOOD OLD FINNISH ROW BOAT   143

THIRTY-ONE: SPECIAL REPORT FROM THE U.S. NAVY   147

THIRTY-TWO: SMALL CRAFT FOR THINKERS   150

THIRTY-THREE: GREY'S BOAT   154

THIRTY-FOUR: ENVIRONMENT   160

THIRTY-FIVE: BUYING THAT SMALL OLD BOAT   164

THIRTY-SIX: RIPPLES IN THE WIND   170

ACKNOWLEDGEMENTS   173

ONE

A KID'S GARDEN OF BOAT BUILDING

Once upon a time (all good tales start this way), Popular Mechanics had a short article on how to build a colossal flat bottom boat to rival the **Queen Mary** or **QEII** with such splendor that the **Titanic** withers in comparison. Cousins Joe and Bill Cunningham discovered this article and consulted with Hegs who had to be the smartest kid to ever walk the streets of Waukon, Iowa. Immediately they decreed that such a vessel must be built and commenced collecting peach crates, plywood, hammers, saws, and nails, and anything else that looked like it should be around a junk yard, I mean ah; boat yard.

The first corporate decision was to turn the area behind Cunningham's house and Dee Hasting's cornfield into an industrial site. In other words, this was the repository of all the brain power, paraphernalia, wood, old Playboys, cigarettes, tools, and boys required to build such a piece of art. Please note that Dee Hastings's cornfield was very important to young boys. It served as a quick place to pee, smoke a sinful cigarette (actually a cigarette was to be shared by at least eight boys), or look at a well-worn 1959 edition with the spectacular Miss November who in those days left more covered than uncovered. All were worthy of a trip to the Saturday afternoon confessional.

The flat-bottom Jon boat was crafted with great deliberation and as much skill as a bunch of pre-teens could muster. We had not discovered the delights of fiberglass or resin so the concept of sealing the seams was based pretty much on using more nails. It was designed for the use of two people so in our mind that meant at least four or maybe five boys. Lacking paint, we went au natural although we may have splashed on a little varnish or some other coating if there was any lying around in the Cunningham basement. Itch A'hearn joined us with no desire for labor. For the record and with the sense of full disclosure I admit that I stood around a watched Joe, Bill, and Jim do all the work. It was messy and mom wouldn't approve of my getting my clothes dirty. Further, hammering a nail or sawing a straight line was far, far beyond my abilities. I honestly believe the Y chromosome for woodworking and carpentry totally missed me. My father and my son are pretty good at that sort of thing but I remain hopelessly challenged, as the politically correct folk say.

We quickly requested an adult to take several of us boys and the boat to Yellow River to make a test run. In the minds of a 12-year-old, a test run and a full-blown cruise were pretty much the same. Mr. Cunningham nicely volunteered to haul boat, boys, and assorted necessities such as food, pop, and oars. Except the oars resembled 1x4s left over from some project.

Leo left us off by a bridge and said he would pick us up at another bridge a few hours later. Off he went. We sailors and nautical architects pushed the boat down the bank and into the water. So, the crew of 5 plopped into the boat and shoved off. Joe immediately seized command as Captain and Skipper; Bill, being co-owner of the boatyard, expected to be the Second in Command; Hegs, the brains of the outfit assumed the position of Naval Architect and Chief Engineer; and Itch and I became Feeble Bodied Seamen.

Immediately some obvious design defects became apparent. The weight in the boat seemed to be greater than our mathematical computations; therefore, the water was approximately 1 inch from the gunnels and the right beam corner was dead even with the river. Mere breathing caused that corner to dip underneath the water and great quantities of water gushed into the hull. By shifting weight, holding our breath, and paddling gingerly we could almost remain afloat. Well, afloat only if Itch bailed like crazy. Engineer Hegs and Skipper Joe instantly commanded that the smallest Seaman be assigned to the problematic corner. Being the youngest and smallest I sat for the entire voyage with my rump submerged. My saturated pants and underwear rapidly created an itch that no scratch could ameliorate. It became paddle, paddle, and scratch, scratch, and paddle some more. Our only hope for survival rested in the solemn belief that increased speed would create outflow of water, would keep more water from entering the boat, and, if nothing else, hurry our adventure so we could disembark. I remember watching our lunch float away but we needed to keep up paddling pace to avoid catastrophe.

Struggling to our fullest, some genius decided the boat was errant because it lacked a proper name. No doubt the esteemed Hegs, who was unquestionably the smartest we ever knew, proffered this particular concept. We all recognized Hegs as the resident scholar and philosopher, and we readily agreed.

After some contemplative debate, suggested ideas, and discourse on appropriate names, we turned to Captain Joe (the whole boat thing was his idea anyway), for official and mandatory approval. We came up with **THRESHER** after the nuclear submarine that sank with all hands. We fully agreed that it was a good, proper, and appropriately nautical name. Captain Joe concurred, and **THRESHER** it was.

The **THRESHER** eventually reached the appointed bridge after sinking several times. A grateful crew thanked God that the Yellow River was so shallow. The boat was full of water and thoroughly water logged making it neigh on impossible to turn over to dump our watery contents. Leo was waiting for us and said nary a word about five muddy and soaked water rats that passed as the crew.

I do believe that the **THRESHER** made only that one voyage. Certainly, I was never aboard her again, and I am surprised that mom let me go in the first place. On the other hand, it might have slipped my mind asking permission. Mom's consistent response to all requests was a pointed, "NO!" I wasn't totally ignorant so asking mom for anything usually never occurred.

THRESHER no doubt was salvaged and turned into a wooden Go-Cart or fort or tree house. Wood never was wasted and was used until a board had more nail holes than wood. Over fifty years later this magnificent boat remains a topic of reminiscence over a few beers whenever we get together, which isn't often. Skipper Joe went on to become a pharmacist and take over my dad's drug store. Bill, a gifted student who thought things like homework impeded his acquisition of knowledge, tragically died in an accident. I doubt if anyone has seen Itch in years. Dr. Hegs teaches at the Med School and the Law School at the University of Iowa while practicing medicine and law in rural Iowa, and he remains the smartest kid I ever knew. I am old, retired, and in love with my West Wight Potter **"Genny Sea"**. Love of the water was born one summer day on the Yellow River in Iowa onboard a Jon boat named **Thresher**, and it has never waned.

TWO

DRIFTLESS ZONE

Mother Nature, in all her glory and wisdom, compensated Middle America for her glaciers that flattened the region eventually yielding wonderful cropland by skipping a stretch of land and allowing it to remain rugged, wild, and wonderful. Modern geologists call this the Driftless Area, but the Ioway and other Native American tribes called it the Ocooch Mountains. The great glaciers of the Paleozoic failed to cover a region of 24,000 square miles along the Mississippi River in Southeastern Minnesota, South Western Wisconsin, and Northeast Iowa. As the ice melted, the enormous quantity of water carved massive valleys with bluffs ranging from 600 to 1700 feet. This geological event set the stage for the great hardwood forests of Middle America. It also established some of the most beautiful rivers in the United States.

Stretching from Lake Pepin, the widest spot of the Mississippi, to Dubuque, the Driftless Area possesses rivers and streams unmatched outside of mountain ranges. It proffers canoers and kayakers a pristine, clear water view of an area much as it existed eons ago with high bluffs, forests, and limited intrusion by humans. The streams teem with Brook, Rainbow, and Brown trout that until 40 years ago were all native to their creeks. Now the trout are stocked by the various states. The rivers boast a plethora of species of fish including pan fish like the sunfish, perch, bluegill, crappies, and bullheads. The area is home to gar, paddlefish, Largemouth and Smallmouth bass, sauger, walleye, and northern. The mussels have been a special concern for outdoors people. The rare and endangered Higgins's Eye and winged maple leaf clam live around small beds highly protected by the DNR. Unfortunately, the invasive and prodigious Zebra clam has caused significant damage to urban wells, freshwater intake systems, and storm sewer outflows to say nothing of wreaking havoc on the endangered species in the region. Overall, there are 28 varieties of mussels in the Driftless Area.

As the various glaciers melted the tremendous volume of water rushing at a torrid rate flooded the Mississippi River to about 163 feet deeper than present day. University of Minnesota geologists maintain the River Warren Falls near today's St. Paul, MN would make Niagara Falls look like a ripple. Lake Agassiz, a monstrous inland lake formed from the glacial waters was about the size of the Black Sea. This fed the Mississippi.

DRIFTLESS ZONE

For the modern-day traveler, the Driftless Area is a prime opportunity to view an American region unlike any other. The high and heavily forested bluffs are wonders when seen from either above or at water level. Plenty of options are available for everyone.

The Driftless Area starts at Lake Pepin, about 60 miles downriver from St. Paul, MN. The lake is approximately 40 square miles of water with an average depth of 21. It is the home for boats of all sizes. Sailboats with a waterline of over 40 feet can sail comfortably and have all the facilities usually found on the Great Lakes. Outside the main channel kayaks, canoes, small sailboats, and dinghies have copious space to enjoy. A plethora of motels and restaurants line the lake on both sides. If you watch the Walter Matthau/ Jack Lemon movie, GRUMPY OLD MEN, you will recognize the area where it was filmed in Wabasha. All the little towns on both sides of the river proffer many regional indicative shops, antique shops, and river themed stores.

The 6,000 streams and rivers flow through the Driftless Area allowing a virtually infinite series of canoe and kayak trips. Fishing from the river banks, out in the channel, or in sloughs is prodigious and interesting, especially if the person were to watch closely for wildlife ranging including coyotes, muskrats, beavers, deer, otters, and even an occasional bear. Trails have erupted all over the zone and hikers have become a major economic boon. Bikers are found on every backroad and highway.

Between 800 and 1600 years ago, Indians of various tribes, started burying their dead in mounds located on bluff tops along the Mississippi. Originally, the mounds were round and shaped like upturned bowls. Sometime in the middle of the mound building period, they shifted to animal shaped mounds. Many of the mounds are shaped like birds and bears. Over the hundreds of years before European trappers arrived, virtually every bluff along the river had at least one burial mound.

The most attractive and accessible of these mounds are at Effigy Mounds National Park near Marquette, Iowa where rangers will provide a running commentary as they guide you along the paths. These guides will point out a multitude of wild berries, plants, and flowers and discuss how they were used by the region's inhabitants. Unfortunately, they will also note that the Driftless Area was the transition between the great hardwood forests and the relatively flat plains. During the late 19th and early 20th centuries, strip-logging for the valuable oaks, hickory, ash, and walnut left the forest bare. Slow growing, these hardwoods were elbowed out by meandering, fast growing, and invasive maples. Today's forests are predominately maple but remnants of the hardwoods can be found.

Once the significance of Effigy Mounds was recognized, naturalists created a myriad of parks protecting the bluffs and establishing timberland similar to the area's original plant life. Their efforts are seen each fall as the trees turn a rainbow of yellows, reds, oranges, and shades of green that attract tourists from across the nation. An autumn tour of Allamakee and Clayton counties in Iowa, the river roads of Southeastern Minnesota, and the coulee region of Wisconsin should be a bucket-list dream.

THREE

FEATS

Every sailor has a story about who sparked their interest in boats and water. Each tale is interesting to tell and equally appealing to hear. For some, it was a parent or neighbor or old salt that conned them into jumping aboard their Jon boat or fishing boat or dinghy to spend some time with the Gods of the Waters. So here is my story.

Doc Wheat was a North Dakota boy who violated the typical paths of males during the early 20's; he attended high school instead of scratching out a meager living if not bare subsistence on the farm. In an era when self-sufficiency was the norm and a whole pen of hogs garnished a mere couple of bucks, women tilled vegetable gardens while the men planted and cut hay. Canning the fruits of their gardens and salting a bit of pork or beef sustained the family through the year. Hard currency was uncommon and difficult to attain. Roy Wheat, in spite of the Germanic vexations of his mother, continued his education with the intent of entering dentistry, an unbelievable endeavor and a pipe dream according to the family. Worse, the Dakotas did not have a College of Dentistry and enrollment at the University of Minnesota was limited. While his mother carped about being too big for his britches, Roy travelled to Iowa City, IA from the plains of Hope, North Dakota in search of a dream. The few demeaning letters sent by his mother remained in his office desk throughout his life.

Upon graduation, Wheat surveyed Iowa and realized that the railroad crossroads of Marquette, IA, across the river from Prairie du Chien, Wisconsin had numerous itinerant railroad workers travelling through the town but no dentists. He immediately opened his office above a tavern called the Bucket of Blood. His first day he pulled 72 teeth even when one brutish railroad worker warned him that if the extraction hurt, he was going to toss the newly minted dentist out of the second story window. Evidently, it was painless.

Two concepts flourished as he established his practice on the Mississippi River: he could make a decent living working on people's teeth and he could find pleasure at the river. Soon he opened offices in nearby Waterville, Iowa and the county seat, Waukon, riding the train for 50 cents. He also started fishing the Mississippi river and the many trout streams running along the bluffs before disgorging the clear waters into Old Muddy.

Doc finally purchased an old aluminum boat with an equally ancient Johnson motor and kept them at the Wayne Wines boat yard in Harpers Ferry, which was indeed just a yard in front of Wayne's old decrepit shack. Wayne fashioned a bunch of washing machine rollers and a winch to a frame so Doc could pull his boat ashore without much strain. Doc always treated Wayne with kindness and dignity but from the paucity of teeth in Mr. Wines' mouth it could be assumed that he was not a patient.

I know I was fairly young when I first commenced my voyages with Doc, and it was I who gave him the name "Feats". Evidently my brain function as a small child did not provide a schema whereby my mother could address my dad as "dad", and her father – Doc – could also be "dad". The solution was to proffer a name "Daddy Wheat" to my grandfather. My blithe little tongue could only mutter "Daddy Feat". It rapidly became just plain old Feats, and it was by this name he remained until his death. My grandmother's name was Zonona and she became Nanny. Nanny and Feats became the two most wonderful people in my world and would be for a half a century.

They lived just three doors away in the quaint little Iowa town of Waukon, the county seat of Allamakee County. The county was named after explorer Allan McKee who was among the first White trappers in the area. The French established Prairie du Chien, Wisconsin in the late 1600's as a trading post for mountain men of legend to trade furs for necessary goods. The local Sac and Fox slurred his name as Allamakee, and that remained when they named the county.

Feats loved the river, as much as the Indians who lived along its banks even when I was a small boy. He would occasionally stop to chat with Emma Big Bear who stood on a corner in Marquette selling homemade baskets (he should have bought a bunch because they are worth small fortunes today). He would invariably take me along on his fishing excursions as soon as I was old enough to don a life vest that was made of stale smelling canvas and kapok. We would sit for hours drowning worms with sincere hope that a bluegill or sunfish would commit suicide by impaling itself on our hooks.

The river town of Lansing built a small marina. Doc had always kept his little fishing boat at Harpers Ferry that was merely two taverns, a church, a couple of houses, and a general store. You could have purchased the entire town and surrounding acres for a few hundred dollars. However, in recent years the city folk have re-discovered Harpers Ferry and a speck of land large enough to build a small cabin sells for $30,000 today. A condo there will suck you dry for around 200 thousand bucks. Obviously, Feats had little foresight and less investment astuteness.

Doc sold his boat and purchased a much larger Lone Star runabout with a 50 horsepower Evinrude (the largest motor at the time was a 75 horse Merc). His high-sided boat made my parents a little happier, and the marina made it easier for Feats to dock. Furthermore, the kind marina operators sold gas and provided repair service, for a fee. The local gossip, blarney and bad jokes were free.

So, every Thursday afternoon and Sunday Doc could be found on the river. Nanny was less than exuberant about the river complete with drunken fisherman and barges; but I suspect that the stout lady found boarding and unboarding difficult and the ride less than comfortable to say little about the heat and humidity that Iowa corn loves but her people detest. Preferring an able-bodied crew, Feat would consistently ask me to ride along.

The routine was invariably the same. We would load up his Buick with the requisite safety equipment, a cooler of beer and pop, and some worms in case we decided to fish. Entering Lansing we would stop at Gaunitz Meat Market to buy a ring of bologna or summer sausage. We would take off from the marina and my job was to wait for Feats to attain full speed at which time I would open the pit cock and drain whatever water was on the deck. Then we would find a slough to fish. Catch a fish, clean a fish, cut off a piece of bologna with the same knife, and drink Nehi Strawberry pop while Feats did the same with a cold Hamm's beer from the Land of Ski Blue Waters.

I greatly loved Feats and he imparted the ways of the waters for me. Those had to be the best times ever. But it was the whole experience of a trip to the river that mattered. It was the exchange of jokes and gossip, the bologna and pop, and the teasing of the river guys that hung around the marina. Great stories emanated from those adventures.

After every grand voyage Doc would stop at Sweeney's Tavern for one small glass of beer to lie about the number and size of the fish we caught, complain about whatever was the complaint of the day, catch up on old friendships, and gab about nothing of importance but essential to life on the river.

One day one of the bar regulars was deep into his beer and in immense pain from an infected tooth. Doc told him to come up to the office the next day and he'd administer to it. "Oh no," the local whined, "You damn dentists charge too much." Still, he moaned and groaned in awesome agony. Clearly, everyone at the bar felt compassion for the old geezer; however, their patience had been tried to their limit. Finally, Doc's patience also reached its zenith. He ordered a shot of Jack Daniels, reached into his tackle box and found a pair of pliers used to skin fish. He walked over to the sufferer, peered into his mouth of blackened teeth, saw the swollen gums around the severely infected tooth, and promptly stuck his pliers into said mouth and extracted the cause of the disturbance. Quietly, he told the drunk to swish with the Jack Daniels and he would be good as new. Sixty years after the fact they still talk about the superior dentistry practiced at Sweeney's Tavern in Lansing.

Feats died suddenly in a fashion that should be replicated by all old boaters. He walked downtown to his office, put in a good day of work, came home and entertained guests for dinner at which time many laughs were had. After good food and good drinks, he said his good byes to his friends. He sat down on his bed, smoked a good cigar, and quietly died of a stroke.

Doc Wheat has been gone for a long, long time but his memory still lingers around the river. Old people still tell me about their dentures created by my grandfather. Sometimes they even pull them out to show me. Some may find such display as gross and unpleasant but I know river people, know Doc's pride in his craftsmanship, and appreciate their respect.

THE WORLD'S WORST SAILOR

Sweeney's Tavern still stands in Lansing overlooking the Mississippi. It is a great place to view the barges and traffic, to hear bad jokes and gossip, and to mellow out on a cold beer. If you listen well, you may be fortunate enough to hear the old timers talk about fish, boats, floods, and a story about a dentist who loved the river.

FOUR

I GOT DA BLUES

Reaching retirement age and brimming with dreams set aside for such a time, I decided to purchase my first sailboat. After careful research I fell in love with a Boatex 1200 dinghy, and I called the esteemed Roger Poole, owner of Boatex and son of the famed designer Aaron Poole, and made my order. Roger is a pretty nice guy and offered me copious options including a nice colored stripe on the hull and matching color in the sail. He said blue was the fashion hue of the season. But his statement brought me to the keen awareness that I was about to drift into an area far beyond the capability of my meager intelligence and personality. Roger said, "What color blue?" Ignorant Doc thought that blue was blue. "Oh no." said Roger, "We have several shades of blue". I knew for certain that I was in trouble.

During my generation's war I joined the American Yacht Club, better known as the U.S. Navy (well, my WWII Marine Corps combat veteran father did imply something about enlist or be left out of the Will). Uniform colors in the Navy were simple: blue and white. Our dress blues were Navy Blue as were out undress blues, our pea coats, and our underwear when we inadvertently tossed our socks in the washing machine with our skivvies after a scholarly night of research and experimentation of pick-up lines on San Diego women at any place that sold alcohol.

In Viet Name we never, ever made mistakes or experienced failures. We had major successes and minor successes. So, when my wife, Miss Kalevala and Goddess of the Lapland, questioned the shade of blue on my sailboat I went to Wal-Mart and checked out crayons to see if blue had somehow changed.

Perhaps I should start by saying that I went to a Catholic elementary school. Because most of the kids came from blue-collar homes and no one had any money, crayons were limited to the 8 per pack size. Additional colors were considered gaudy, immoderate, excessive, showy, and sinful (no doubt mortal). We didn't want to go to hell so we stuck to the Basic Colors. The all-you-ever-need-to-know-about-color Crayola package: black, white, red, yellow, green, blue, orange, and purple. Period.

What color blue? Blue's blue. Well, there might be a dark blue, light blue and blue blue but what heck else could there be? This was a silly question as I was about to find out. Blue just isn't blue anymore. Some loony person (no doubt a WASP, East Coast, art major who had never served in the military, been to Dorchester, or even know of parochial schools) had invented a whole batch of new blues, the likes of which confused and confounded me.

My studies at Drake, Muscatine, Upper Iowa, Winona State, the University of South Dakota, and the Defense Language Institute never covered the concept of "blue". Physics was not my favorite class, in fact, they tossed me out of school before I took it; nevertheless, I did not know that there was a class of hardness to blue. How could blue be hard? But the clerk showed me Soft China blue, Light China blue, Soft Blue, Light Cobalt, Light Aqua, Steel Blue, and Soft Steel Blue (too much lead?). I had an artistic feeling not unlike being stuck in irons. If Diamond blue is tougher than Lodestar or Sapphire or Crystal blue then is Tile Blue weaker? I stupidly asked if there was a heavy blue, and that statement was met with an icy blue stare.

Dumb old me honestly thought blue was blue. The last geography class I took was in 1961 but now we have China Blue (dimwitted me, I thought China was Red!), Emerald blue (I am Irish: isn't the Emerald Isle green?), Aegean Blue (sounds nice and warm to me on a wintry day in Iowa), Blue Ridge (that I thought were mountains), Sausalito blue, Yorktown blue (yes, the British soldiers were pretty blue at Yorktown), Boundary Waters, Delta (yet again dense me thought Delta Blues was music), and Bering Sea (a little colder than Baltic blue perhaps). I stumbled and fumbled at the discovery of Monterey blue and Monterey Bay blue. I lived in Monterey for a year and it is truly a colorful city as well described in the sundry John Steinbeck books. Shocking pink or maybe red but blue and Monterey don't correlate with me. Of course, there is Flemish blue, Erie Canal blue, and French blue. I disliked French classes in college but the Navy made me a French linguist. I take pride in the fact that I scored the lowest on my French finals than anyone in the history of the Defense Department. Madame Dupuis shouted at me, "Monsieur Regan, don't you know ANYTHING?" Yeah, I do: I don't like French and I won't like French Blue either.

My intent on looking nautical took a severe hit when my mind was further bombarded with the fact that blue is a botanical notion. I was confronted Heather blue, Sage blue, Azure Heather, Pool Blue Heather, Blue Iris, Flax Flower blue, Dutch Blue Iris (the damn Dutch always were persnickety but not as bad as the French), Blue Aster, Periwinkle, Floral blue, Bright Blue Heather, Sea Blue Heather, Lapis blue (I thought lapis was a funny name for a rabbit, Thistle blue (when I sit in thistles they are invariably green but I am not about to argue at this point), and Wild Iris (wasn't she a stripper in San Diego?). I never like vegetables and never, ever consider eating something blue, Blue is blue, besides isn't Periwinkle and Iris kind of sissy sounding. What God-fearing sailor who wants to go down to the sea again asking for a tall ship and a star to steer her by would be caught dead in a Floral blue uniform with Blue Iris trousers!

Then my cerebral cortex was really tossed for a loop when introduced to even more blues. There is a Dusk blue (is there a Sunrise Blue?), Sky blue (I remember that Hamm's beer is from the land of sky-blue water), Fresh blue (God help us with a blue that isn't fresh), True blue (never worn by lawyers), Bright blue (talented and gifted?). Bright Blue Heather (must be a female version; is there a Bright Blue Bob?), Clear blue (can cloudy blue be far behind?), Windy blue, Stratosphere blue, washed blue (I'll bet his mother made him wash behind his ears), and Rinsed Blue (well, if you wash you better rinse too). Alpha Blue must be the top dog of blues, and God only knows why the world needs Nimble blue. Crescendo is too loud for my likes, and Blue mood is what I see my shrink for. Blue dream usually involves beautiful bikini clad Scandinavian blondes that give off Blue Flame passions.

Did you know that age makes a difference in blues also? Yuppers, we have an Antique blue and Antique Indigo, Weathered blue and light Antique Indigo. I know that I am old and wearing an old color is not going to attract those gorgeous Scandinavian blonde sweeties to my dockside. On the opposite tack is Baby Blue and Powder blue which are clearly too immature for me. Is there possibly a Middle-Aged Stud Muffin blue?

Water blues were next in line. I looked at Sea blue and Light Sea blue. Saltwater blue must be different than Lake blue. The last time someone said something about colors having a salty taste there were quite high on LSD. Nautical blues come in Navy blue, True Navy blue, Admiral blue (oh, I think that is the one for an old salt like me), Captain's Walk (for those who didn't get their star?), Flag blue, and Marine blue (dad would have liked that one) and Bright Marine blue (for those smart enough not to be grunts?) and even a Deep Ultramarine (that must be for the rally Gung Ho Marines). Bayside blue? Is there a the-head-is-stopped-up-and-we-are-up-to-our-tushes-in-toilet-water blue? Can dockside blue, out in the middle of the Channel blue, and a you-are-locked-in-irons blue also be on the list? What, pray tell, is the difference among Blue mist, Tidal Blue, Seashore, or Lagoon blue? I spent my boyhood in the Mississippi sloughs so there just has to be a Mississippi Backwater blue. I can't imagine how Shifting Wave blue is different than Southern Sea, Trout Stream, Sea Galleon, Blue Ocean, or 7 Lakes blue. In the water line we also have Seaside blue, Blue Wave, Portal blue, Blue Ocean, and Transatlantic. You know there is a Pacific blue, Mediterranean, Arctic, and Caribbean blue somewhere.

I was given a B.A. degree at Upper Iowa University (anything to get rid of me). We were the Upper Iowa Peacocks (cheering "Go Peacocks, Fight" hardly struck terror in the hearts of the Luther Norsemen or Wartburg Knights). I think Peacock blue is a bit loud. Worse, the official color of the university is not Peacock blue but actually Columbia blue. Do bluebloods at Columbia wear Royal blue? All I recognize is that when in Navy boot camp we wore Chambray blue shirts. Bluebirds used to poop on our parade grinder. "Bluebirds" was the best reading group in First Grade (I was in Redbirds until Sister Mary Annette sent me down to the Crows). We do have the choice among Bluebird blue, Parrot, Robin's Egg, Jay, and Bird's Eye. Don't ask me to tell you the difference between Peacock and Peacock Plume blue.

You must not be anybody unless you have a blue named after you. Holly must be a tribute to Buddy Holly who died here in Iowa. Chopin and Caruso blues are candidates from the classical music department. Picasso and Degas represent painter. Cornelia blue must be named after the wild Irish woman who rode roughshod over the Sisters of the Presentation of Virgin Mary. For the record, Sister Mary Cornelia was my great aunt. Electra and Neptune come out of the blue of Mount Olympus. Blue Phantom a slight nod towards the stage musical?

In the end I told Mr. Poole to send my little dinghy in the blue he liked best. I am sorry I have had enough blue until I am red in the face. Oh dear Lord, lets no go there.

FIVE

MY FIRST YEAR SAILING

Growing up in the seafaring state of Iowa I was entranced by the waves of golden grain, the white caps on the farm ponds, and the sandy beaches along the creek beds. Like most Iowa boys my dreams of a cruiser with billowing spinnaker knifing through the blue waters of St. Kitts (wherever the heck that is) with a crew of bikini clad blondes sunning on the decks, engulfed my waking moments, especially in Inorganic Chemistry and Calculus classes. The fantasy furthered when I was invited to sail on **8's ENOUGH,** a 30 foot Mega, off the Apostle Islands in Lake Superior. Later I spent a day on a remodeled Morgan, **CatchinSun**. I subscribed to Latitudes and Attitudes, Good Old Boat, and Messing Around in Boats, and I was hooked.

My first act of retirement, after signing up for my retirement pension, was to spend a plethora of hours procrastinating from my daily HONEY-DO chores to ply the waves of the Internet looking for the perfect boat. I settled between two pretty good dinghies: a Sun Chaser II and a Boatex 1200. The latter was selected because I liked the idea of a boat built one at a time by the world-renowned builder, Roger Poole (that's what the ad said).

April 1 2003, I called the eminent Mr. Poole in Canada and ordered my boat, which he said would take 4 weeks to build and ship to Iowa. By

May 1 I was in acute anxiety over the non-delivery of said dinghy and the plethora of phone exchanges between Canada and the U.S. (no doubt monitored by the National Security Agency with reports going to the CIA and the National Rifle Association) offered no relief. Unexpected impedance to my fantasy came in the guise of one President George

W. Bush. He obviously and clearly became aware of the fact that I voted for Gore, and he instituted -- just to screw me over-- a whole bundle of Homeland Security orders with the firm intent on barring any boat made in Canada from entering the United States of America. The forms and documents and sundry legal blarney (I am Irish and I do know blarney when I see it or hear it: I am also an Iowa boy who knows bull... well we won't go there either) made the boat's border crossing neigh on impossible. Worse, the hassle on the truckers made crossing the border an unprofitable trip so the cost of transportation into the U.S. was more than the cost of the boat itself.

Finally, after much complaint and calling in all political IOU's that I had in my pocket, the boat was loaded onto a truck to be in Iowa within 24 hours. Both Mr. Poole and I had forgotten that along with all the bureaucracy piled higher and deeper by the administration, the President had created a whole battalion of new border guards replete with badges, guns, night sticks, mace spray, walkie-talkies, tire puncture devices, stun guns, stun grenades, smoke bombs, sawed-off shot guns, and a damn good case of "attitude".

Most of these gendarmes are under 20 years old, graduated at the bottom of their high school classes, and see all Northern Pike and Muskie as a clear and present danger to the continuation of the American Way of Life. Boats in a truck clearly are disguised weapons of mass destruction designed by those cleaver terrorists from the Mideast. The trucker was forced into a 24-hour interrogation about the boat, the design, the purpose of it, and why was it bound for Iowa when everyone knows there is no water in Iowa. Worse, he was born and raised in Texas but now lives in Canada (obvious evidence of a terrorist because who would ever think of 'leaving" the beloved U.S. of A).

Nevertheless, the perseverance of the ex-Texan driver and more wits the guards at the border he entered the U.S. He said that you should have seen Home Security Militia measuring all fish, checking all camping gear, and inspecting creels and reels of the fishermen. These border guards, evidently, didn't know that some Americans go to Canada to fish.

In July the fantasy craft arrived at my driveway thanks to a courteous phone call from the trucker telling me exactly when he would be in Cedar Rapids if I could give him directions from I-380. My beauty was packed in a 2x4 lumber casing and enough Styrofoam to float New Jersey. The afternoon was spent in the delicate and deliberate operation of extracting the dinghy from it protective shell. There it stood: a boat, a mast, a boom, a rudder, a center board, a pail of sails, and a whole bunch of colored line. Unfortunately for a beginner, I could find nothing resembling a manual on how to rig this thing. As I always have done when encountering such ventures, I waited until the next day, looked at a photo, drank a 6 pack of Miller Genuine Draft, and hoisted the sails.

Being an intelligent person with several college degrees, I reckoned that the best way to learn sailing is through a thorough understanding of the concept via reading. A good sailing book and a secreted volume of **Sailing for Dummies** were purchased, the pictures viewed, and the editions placed in a highly visual spot on the living room coffee table for all to see.

Once in the water I discovered the true beauty of sailing one's own boat. However, the Boatex 1200 seemed to be missing something. A decal for the stern provided the name: **ZONONA** Since I was now a true sailor I, of course, needed new togs which included a cap from *LATTITUDES AND ATTITUDES,* sailing pants (the quick dry type), monogrammed shirts bearing the foul anchor and **ZONONA** emblazoned on the chest, and an expensive pair of boat shoes.

After brother Mikey and I made a couple of trips to the lake together, it was high time to experience a solo voyage. Trying to get the 15-foot mast into place by myself on a windy day proved a modest challenge, especially since I made sure I had parked immediately aside the beach inundated with bikini clad women. Waving around the hunk of aluminum in a stiff breeze I resembled some sort of cartoon character or Jackie Gleason skit. Embarrassed, I set sail and had a reasonable cruise. The sting of the embarrassment entitled me to order new stationery picturing a sailboat and the word **ZONONA**.

Subsequent solo sailing around the little lake was incredibly enjoyable. With a stiff breeze I could handle the main part of the water. It was the little inlets that I discovered that sailboats need wind, and wind does not exist in the little inlets with high banks. After hours of coaxing the boat toward anything that looked like rippling water, I finally swam ashore dragging the boat with a rope in my teeth. I bought a paddle on the way home.

Proclaiming myself a true and experienced skipper, one day I saw that the wind was whipping up furiously. "Aha", said I. "Lots of wind equals lots of speed!" The trailer was immediately attached to the car and I rushed to the lake. With complete comprehension of Physics (although I struggled with it in high school and totally ignored it in college), I decided that if more wind equals more speed than the corollary hold that more wind requires more sail. Therefore, I thought nothing of raising the foresail, pushing off, and trying to raise the mainsail.

I underwent yet another "experiential learning lesson! After shoving off is not the time to check if the rigging is in proper repair and not foul. I lifted the sheet about halfway when the darn thing stuck. When sailing you often have split second decisions to make, and in this case, it was whether to work on the jammed line or man the tiller. In a moment requiring decisive command I opted for the former, figuring that the boat was moving along pretty and could steer herself for a moment. The sail was finally lowered and I had a chance to adjust the direction of my wonderful vessel. Bring a brilliant sailor, the likes of which Patrick O'Brian writes, I headed for a semi-protected inlet where I could work on the problem line. The boat was headed into the less violent waters when I again lofted the mainsail only this time it jammed about three quarters up the mast. A wind, which has not been felt on this earth since the fabled walls of Jericho tumbled before the blast of Joshua's horn, hit my little dinghy. The next conscious moment found me wondering what the heck happened. First, I was standing in the boat and then I was in the water staring at the underside of my hull.

Because my myriad sailing books happened to have a picture of a capsized boat, I utilized my enormous talents to stand on the dagger board and attempt to right the boat, just like in the pictures. If I ever find that photographer or author of the book, I shall probably be charged with assault with intent to deliver serious harm to their well-being. I stood on the boat and struggled trying to upright said boat. Instead, my shoes drifted away with the breeze, my wallet and checkbook popped from my pocket and sank like lead balls, but the dumb boat would not come erect. The more I worked on the boat, the more the mast worked itself into the weeds and the sails acted like a net scooping in tons of weeds, mud, and assorted junk. No amount of weight on the dagger board would right that sucker. Again, pausing to let my intellect and calm demeanor set in, I recognized that I had to" a) point the nose into the wind, b) disconnect the sails which were mired in heavy weeds, and c) pull the mast from the boat. I reasoned, quite logically, that once rid of the sails and mast; the boat would naturally turn upright.

Taking deep breaths, I dove into the slimy water and did indeed unfasten the sails. The next object of my effort was directed toward the mast that was held by a lengthy bolt and wing nut. I disconnected the nut and yanked out the bolt both of which immediately joined my checkbook at the bottom. The mast came out of its seat at the floor of the boat and was almost out of the foredeck when the silly boat decided to roll over again, this time tearing a nice 18-inch hole where the mast used to stand. There I tread in slimy, weedy waters until an elderly man came by with his pontoon boat, gathered in my shoes and sundry floating supplies including the mast and sails. The dagger board must have gotten tangled in the weeds and was not to be found.

No problem. I went to the Internet to find a fiberglass repairman and to order a piece of scrimshaw for the mantle and a new sailor hat. I also asked Mr. Poole to send another dagger board.

After the Dinghy Doctor repaired the boat, I inventoried the many supplies and accessories necessary for a 12-foot dinghy: plastic tote boxes, new sun glasses strap (bright red), more and more lines, a computerized wind speed indicator, a pair of life vests (keep your comments to yourself), and a huge bundle of bungee cords. Realizing the necessity for an anchor I purchased a plastic encased heavy mushroom anchor and 25 feet of cotton rope. This, I thought, should definitely hold me in the future.

My confidence, never at a loss but occasionally less than supreme, rose with each additional venture to the water. Backing a trailer into the lake was soon as easy as pulling into my driveway. Adding a roller at the end of the trailer made loading significantly easier and a lot less of the bow banging into the trailer floor before mounting the padded boards. I was really a good sailor now. Well, there was this once that I was putting the boat in and forgot about the stupid winch handle on the silly winch. As **ZONONA** slipped easily into the water the handle spun like a wheel on a slot machine. It was a surprise of some suddenness when it smacked me cleanly on the nose and exhibiting how much blood could be spewed from a single nasal injury. I pretended not to notice and hung my head near the spot where they clean fish so no one would notice the blood. My face ashen from blood loss did not keep me from sailing. I did avoid coming close to other boats for the remainder of that day. And I I kept away from the lake until the black eyes disappeared.

The next solo included an attempt to anchor in mid channel while I adjusted the rigging so I would not suffer yet another catastrophic mishap. The wind and current assisted me into placing the boat far from any rocks and shoals. The new anchor had been attached to the new line with the best granny knot I could fashion. Navy Boot Camp insisted on trying to instruct us mere swabs with the rudiments of seamanship such as how to abandon ship (I did pay attention as that seemed to be "how to save your own tush" information worthy of retaining), how to effectively use a paint brush (yeah, sure, I stayed awake for THAT lecture), and how to tie knots. Because at that time I held two college degrees, I figured that it would only be a matter of days before Uncle Sam's Canoe Club realized their incredible oversight and would immediately send me to Officer Training School, if not a direct commission to which I was certainly due; therefore, such application knowledge as paint brush care and tying ropes was insignificant and meaningless to one as great as me. The square knot and the bow knot were all that were important.

Having attempted and failed to put a square knot attaching the line to the anchor, my mind affirmed that the dear old granny was more than sufficient. Indeed, it showed that it could hold rather well, if I do say so myself. I tossed the anchor over the side.

Now it never occurred to me that the lake might have depth greater than I anticipated. Ranging from depths of 8 to 30 feet I evidently accidentally drifted into the incredibly small area that was of greater depths. The anchor splashed mightily and sank quickly from sight as the line pulled quickly behind. My next experiential learning moment came when I recognized that when utilizing an anchor two knots are required: one attaching the anchor to the line and, quite interestingly, one attaching the line to some part of the boat. The anchor rode went right over the side into approximately 50 feet of water. Whereupon I learned my second and third lessons of the day: a) make sure you have more anchor line than the distance between the boat and the bottom, and, b) cotton line does not float. My anchor and its shiny white cotton rope disappeared with great speed

Being a well-prepared sailor, I immediately measured off approximately 30 feet of line (a true sailor never has too much line), tied a lead weight to one end and a fluorescent marker to the other so I could mark the spot of the missing anchor. Unfortunately, the boat had drifted some distance from the spot of the loss and equally unfortunate was my measuring system that ended up still short of the bottom. With the drift of the boat and my marker floating quickly away downwind, I had to take a manual WAG as to where on the lake the anchor should be.

Now armed with four (4, count them) college degrees in hand, I knew my intellect would bring forth a rapid and easy means for finding my anchor. First, I invested in a GPS system for future problems, should they ever happen again. Second, I bought a fish depth finder so I could find the anchor in the mud along the bottom.

The depth finder unfortunately didn't do me any good whatsoever. It did allow me some wonderful views of where fish were and where the bottom became cluttered with junk instead of mud, otherwise it was pretty worthless except for the chronic buying of batteries (did I sell that Eveready stock?).

Back to the cognitive drawing board, I purchased a wet suit, mask, fins, snorkel and a really nifty dive watch with hands that glow in the dark. The depth of the lake is not that deep and I am in pretty good shape. Duh, why did I not think of this earlier? All I needed to do was take a deep breath, surface dive, look around, and at least mark the spot of the anchor even if I couldn't bring it up.

The plan was fool proof except for a couple of issues unrecognized in my foolproof planning. My 7 mm Farmer John wet suit is pretty buoyant. Trying to dive in that outfit was next to impossible without many pounds of weights. Strapping a couple of rocks to my belly was an option since lead weights could only be purchased at a dive shop many miles away. Worse, the visibility could be measured in millimeters in spite of an expensive Pelican light I bought with the wet suit. Diving for several days did not provide any view of the anchor. So much for my foolproof planning.

My little brother has never been of similar personality to me. He was the guy who believed that WORK was a means to gain fiscal resources, whining is inappropriate for males, and common sense saves days, nay months of anxiety. I always figured God gave me my amazing intellectual prowess and intuitive mind so his arguments were as flawed as can be. After all, I had a Ph.D. and he only earned a B.A. at UNI (the University of Nothing Important) instead of a great institution like the University of South Dakota. He of Strong-Back versus my Strong-Mind mentality did provide an occasional ear to listen to my sundry plans, providing that my skin was thick enough for his cynical laughs. My brother often says, "It must suck being you." I never did understand what he was talking about.

Brother Michael owns a restaurant. It is at his Country Kitchen that I pour forth my occasional woes while he pours coffee for which I figure I should not pay. His waitresses seem to like me a lot for they often surround me asking for stories of my latest sailing escapades even though the cafe is full of demanding customers. Obviously, my gleaming personality is attractive to the opposite gender.

For Christmas this year Mikey was munificent enough to buy me another anchor. Like a dork, he left on the price tag. It read $14.95.

SIX

MONEY

Ah, such is the innocence of an Iowa scholar whose seafaring experience included four years in the Navy, which, unfortunately, was time split between the Army and the Air Force. The only time I was on a Navy base was for boot camp. I read O'Brian's books, Moby Dick, Two Years before the Mast, and I had written a biography of Admiral Frank Jack Fletcher; therefore, I had all the knowledge I needed to purchase a boat. The Boatex 1200 dinghy arrived, and I felt what more could I possibly need?

Well, there was the need to buy a trailer but since I already had a little utility trailer for moving my daughter back and forth to college, I found a kit to make it into a small boat trailer. I figured the $200 was a wonderful savings. The kit, of course, needed some adjusting to make it work on my trailer so a trip to Carver ACE hardware was needed for the requisite bolts, nuts, and drill bits (they always get lost).

This all worked really nicely except that my boat tended to smack the metal end of the trailer before it hit the skid pads. A quick trip to the local marine dealer found me with a good roller. Another jaunt to Carver ACE hardware for more bolts and bits. But while I was there, I added some line.

The trailer was just right except that the boat trailers have the tires at the rear because that is where all the weight is. My little hermaphrodite had the wheels in the middle and the center of the load made it rear heavy. I scooted to Carver ACE for a couple of sand bags to add up front and I was ready to go.

Dumb ol' me, I forgot that you have to have the boat secured on the trailer so yet another quick drive to Carver ACE (they don't ask for an ID anymore) and I had straps and a whole mess of bungee cords for keeping stuff secured. Of course, I spotted some neat rope and had to purchase some.

I figured that if a guy was going to sail around in the vast lakes of Iowa (OK, a puddle in the middle of a corn field, then), I needed apparel. First was the required boat shoes and a pair of good sandals that just oozed the spirit of sailing, several nice sport shirts with a nautical emblem, a couple of pairs of shorts made of that stuff that dries quickly, and a splendid cap from Latitudes and Attitudes and one from Good Old Boat. I needed a red glasses tube so I wouldn't lose my expensive trifocals (I am old, you know). Cost equaled ...well who paid any attention to that, it ended up on the plastic.

Safety is a chronic and constant issue when sailing. Of course, I added a couple of life jackets, a pair of oars, an anchor and many, many feet of line, and a couple of bumpers so I won't scratch the paint work. Cheap, really cheap. All bought at Wal-Mart. (I can't give all my business to Carver ACE hardware). I was now ready for the greatest voyage since Columbus. Hauling my lovely dinghy to the lake at Palo, I became a true sailor. I had a sailor's collar, I had a sailor's hat, I had a sailor's raincoat, and I had some sailor's shoes. What do you think about that (OK, sorry Dicky Smothers)?

Lessons learned first-hand are lessons well learned. I decided that to keep everything handy, all materials deemed nautical must be placed in, how should I put this, a heap on the deck of the boat. Dinghies, I ascertained, inherently possess a propensity for inversion; therefore, sundry non-floatable objects, as per the Archimedes Law of Displacement, sink like rocks. It takes no great stretch of imagination to recognize that anchors, line, tie-downs, bungee cords, and the like plunge rapidly downward when the boat pretends it's a turtle.

 Another visit to the beloved Carver ACE hardware store (they suggested an ACE card for benefit points), the marine store, and Wal-Mart brought me back to speed quickly.

Realizing that I am a nautical man by nature, I quickly became cognizant that navigation is important. A small GPS system similar to my Yuppie brother's who has ALL the toys and trinkets, augmented by a brilliant flash of ingenuity whereby information regarding depth, speed, water temperature, and whole lots of other stuff could be obtained by an electronic fish finder found its way to my dinghy. Further, a wind gauge was also important after I learned about the tenderness of dinghies. Thank God for Master Card.

When the boat was originally purchased, I bought one of those "Sailing for Really Stupid People" books and videotape showing that even ditzy blondes can sail. I memorized whole passages of the book and watched the tape until it wore out. I was not only an owner of a boat; I now was an expert on sailing.

But sometimes in the excitement of the launch certain "rules" are ignored, not intentionally, mind you, but overlooked nevertheless. The concept of pointing the bow into the wind as you raise the sail or making certain that the mast is stepped correctly or ensuring that the center board is in place happened to be forgotten on April morning. Now Iowa in April is just out of winter. Ice can be found on farm ponds; snow is still in the ditches. Lake water has a temperature slightly above 32 degrees Fahrenheit. So, the captain and master of his ship must be duly warmed with a heavy jacket covered by a windbreaker, tennis shoes made adequate by thick woolen socks, leather gloves, and a warm hat. Of course, when the "rules" are forgotten the tender dinghy not only flips to its side, it turns turtle immediately reconfirming the Law of Displacement yet again scattering anchors, lines, and loads of expensive stuff all over the muddy bottom of the lake. Even more interesting is that the Lord and Master discovered that: a) spring water is pretty darn cold and can take your breath away, b) without breath you panic, c) without air and weighed down with tons of clothes you sink like a brick. Thus ensued the bitter struggle between the weight of waterlogged wool and the mighty kick of a 57-year-old, out of shape ex-dean, professor, and sailor. The laughter from the shore ensured that I made the surface, grabbed the boat which was immediately righted, baled water like it was a Sunday walk in the park, and paddled my boat to the nearest shore where I jumped into my car, dripping wet, peeled off every stitch I had on, set the heater to super high, and put on my best face for the female Park Ranger who came by to see if I was all right. My only problem was a minor little ticket for public nudity at a state park but that didn't cost anything like having to hire a scuba diver to look for my mast that was in 50 feet of water.

Carver ACE hardware gave me a new coffee mug when I restocked. They are really nice people there, in spite of the giggles as I left the store. They even threw in a spindle on which I could wrap my new rode for my newest anchor. And they sold me a lot of fiberglass stuff for me to make a longer and heavier dagger board to replace the one that simply floated away. Furthermore, they fixed my torn screen door to the porch for free. All the clerks know me by name.

I guesstimate that I have about 10,000 feet of line lying on the mud not too far from my fish finder, GPS system, my third anchor (this one a bucket of cement with an eye bolt in it purchased at Carver ACE hardware), my wind indicator, and my mast, boom, and 75 square feet of sail. Unfortunately, the lake is muddy and the visibility is about 6 inches. One of these days I will get some of my stuff back when the Linn County Search and Recovery Team do some training drills. Until then you will find me at Carver ACE hardware or at my desk trying to make my checkbook balance.

And to think I gave up golf to take up sailing because I thought it was cheaper.

SEVEN

ROPE: A FIRST YEAR SAILOR'S BEST FRIEND

My entire life (except for my military years and graduate school) has been spent in Iowa fantasizing about owning a sailboat. Forced retirement smacked me in the face at the ancient age of 55 so I took an in-depth assessment of my life's goals which include round-the-world sailing, winters spent at St. Kitts (wherever the heck that is, but it sounds cool), and luscious bikini clad blonde beauties lounging on my decks, I bought my boat of choice: a Boatex 1200 dinghy. Hey, a guy has to start somewhere.

I was a wonderful member of the Uncle Sam's Yacht Club, occasionally referred to as the U.S. Navy. Trying to avoid the rice paddies of Viet Nam, I volunteered my precious time, talents, and abilities to the Navy shortly after I graduated from college. The Navy, in a moment of unsurpassed inattentiveness, failed to note my exquisite intellect and classified me a Seaman. Instead of Officer Candidate School, the simpletons sent me to boot camp, even though I was convinced that nothing less than a direct commission as at least a Lieutenant Commander was probable. I, therefore, paid little heed to any lessons taught in Recruit Training Camp because I figured it was merely a matter of time before

President Nixon named me Chief of Naval Operations or something. Thus, I slept through marlinspike, and all other sailing-oriented classes. This may have been somewhat of wise choice of the minor variety (remember, during Viet Nam we had no failures, just major and minor successes). Nixon got messed up in Watergate and my command of a battleship never materialized, probably lost in the paper shuffle of the era. Hilary Rodham was an energetic attorney for the impeachment hearings and I blame her directly and personally for the Navy's oversight into my commission.

Many years later I find myself confronted with a 12-foot dinghy complete with mast, boom, sails, and a lot of rope. Stays, lines, halyards, whatever, are all just plain old rope to an old salt like me (I am an old salt and have a Captain's hat which I soaked in salt water to tarnish the gold braid just to prove it). One early discovery is that you just can't have enough rope. Rule #1 is never to pass a hardware or marine store without buying more rope.

You have to have rope to tie the sails to the rope that raises them. You have to have rope to link the big sail to the boom. You have to have lots and lots of rope to keep the boom from lifting, and rope to tie to the rope at the back of the boat so the boom doesn't do 360-degree spins on you. And of course, you need rope to secure the boat while you are launching and berthing. You absolutely must have bumpers of extensive shapes and sizes since you don't want to scratch the paint job, and that too takes a whole assortment of ropes.

No self-respecting sailor worth his grog can possibly sail without an anchor, after all, a foul anchor is the very symbol of our beloved Navy to say nothing of yacht clubs, magazine covers, and innumerable wannabe sailor's tattoos. Anchors need rope. And after you toss the anchor over the side and realize that you forgot to tie the dumb rope to the boat, you get to buy another anchor and some more rope. Then after the Granny knot works out and the anchor again separates from the

ROPE: A FIRST YEAR SAILOR'S BEST FRIEND

boat, you need more of the good cotton stuff that does not float. (I never did get that knot tying stuff down since I slept through that class in boot camp; besides, I was certain that my appointment as Secretary of the Navy was but days away). I suggest buying rope by the spool.

The boat needs to be tied to that wooden thing, you know, a dock or whatever they call it. This mandates ropes of prolific sizes and lengths and colors (we just have to be color conscious and coordinated when sailing or else the Queer Eye for the Straight Guy show will take over my boat. Discussion of appropriate sailing apparel will be discussed in a future article). Color is an imperative concept. Matching rope with the color strip in the sail just makes good sense. Personally, I prefer to show my patriotism with generous use of red, white, and blue ropes and some that are in contrasting colors like orange and purple. This exigency requires lots of ropes (see Rule #1).

I now have a myriad of ropes of copious dimensions and lengths. Further, I have purchased duplicates of all the ropes in case I need them. The easiest place to store all this stuff is on the floor of the boat (I slept through Naval Terms too but I did purchase a really nice coffee table book called Naval Terms Dictionary...I wonder where I put that thing?). In the movies, ropes are all hung on some sort of peg or something or they are all coiled in a circle. I never do that because I can never get the darn things uncoiled in an emergency. The preference is to place the ropes on top of each other. Coiling just makes backlashes that look like my spinning reel after a hard day of bass fishing.

If, and that is a big if, when you are as good a sailor as me, you should happen to turn turtle with the dinghy, all the rope lain in a heap on the deck will coagulate into one pretty large sized mess of cotton and immediately sink to the bottom. This is where the idea of heaping your rope shows its merit. All you have to do is mark the spot with something that floats...usually my hat, go to town and get more rope and some large hooks. Toss the hooked rope over the side and WHAM you'll snag all that rope in a flash. It has worked for me many times.

At this point I should say that obtaining an Ace Hardware card is important. Ace has lots and lots of rope and you can get a discount after a while. At the end of the year, they send you nice little notes and coupons for more rope. They just love me at my neighborhood Ace hardware.

Never get that fancy-schmancy nylon rope because it just dries out and gives you nasty little plastic splinters. Besides I did hear an honest to God U.S. Navy Master Chief Bo' suns Mate say you should use cotton ropes or lines or whatever he called them. He said something about Manila but I think he was talking about a couple girls he met over a San Miguel beer in the P.I. Nope, nothing but good old-fashioned cotton (albeit many colored) rope for my boat. I learned the hard way that length of rope is really important. My first anchor rope was 25 feet long and I tossed the old wedge over the side and promptly took a nap. When I awakened, I discovered I was in the middle of the lake. It seems that the bottom where I tossed my anchor was about 30 feet down and I just sort of floated away. I suggest nothing less than 100 feet of rope for everything, especially if you capsize (see above).

Now that I have the rope thing down to an art form, I can concentrate on the requisite clothing, nautical attire -- both formal and informal-- and the current fashions of a true old salt sailing buff. If you need further instruction on the joy of rope, call me on the cell phone. I am at the lake looking for my mast that is at the bottom somewhere. I'll bet it is close to where I lost my anchor.

EIGHT

GODS OF WIND AND SEA

John Vigor, great sailor and writer, wrote a rather interesting book on how to re-name your boat. It was filled with appropriate rituals, ceremonies, services, offerings and observances necessary to appease the Gods of Wind and the Seas whom we do not wish to insult, offend or affront. Even sailors who publicly display their affinity to recognizable religions and are sailors, tend to be superstitious around boats. We avoid cruising on Fridays, place coins under our masts, ban bananas, and baptize our vessels with champagne (or beer for us inland folks).

From Māori to Mayans, all civilizations have proffered sacrifice and honor to God of the Wind and Waves. Most of us are familiar with the Greek God Aeolus, the keeper of the winds. Homer made sure to include him in his stories or face the wrath of such a god. Odysseus was given a bag of wind (reminds me of one of the guys at the Tic Toc Tap) by this son of Hippotes. Unfortunately, our hero's crew thought it contained gold and riches, opened the bag, and winds blew them all over the Mediterranean. Perhaps this is one of the reasons that crew members should never, ever question the captain's orders.

The Greeks weren't about to slight a god when it came to sailing around the islands. They ensured that winds from each direction had a specific god to appease. Boreas was the god in charge of North winds and of winter. Iowans have not paid heed to Boreas and we have had miserable winters and damn cold Northern gales to show for it. His image is found on various pieces of porcelain as a god wearing a tunic and with wild hair and spikey beard (as if frozen). This is not unlike Iowa fraternity boys running across campus to a toga party.

Eurus handled the breezes from the East. Evidently, he was in charge of storms and foul weather; however, he is also considered the Savior of Sparta. Turbulent seas and storm-tossed boats meant many a Greek pleading with Eurus for mercy.

Zephyrus headed the west and tropical winds and is remembered in our language as zephyr, meaning gentle, warm breezes. Obviously, he was a highly regarded god and important for sailors of the Wine Dark Seas. The poor dude had many wives including Iris the goddess of the rainbow and Chloris who was really in love with his brother Boreas. Greek gods had interesting sexual appetites and they could change themselves as necessary to sire offspring. He also had a blistering affair with Hyacinth. Remembering Leda and the Swan where the poor girl was raped by Zeus in the form of a bird, Zephyrus managed to sire Achilles' horses. And you thought the 1960's were wild.

Notus (that was also the standard reply to Sr. Marie Therese when she asked, "Who did this?") chaired the Department of South winds. His tropical air brought late summer storms that flattened crops. The wine makers feared him because he brought those sirocco winds. The Romans named him Auster and from that the island continent Australia is known. Virgil wrote about him:

> *Just as when a flame falls on the standing grain while the South Winds rage,*
> *or a rushing mountain stream lays low the fields,*
> *lays low the glad crops and labors of oxen,*
> *and drags down forests headlong.*

Egyptians had their own sets of Wind Gods but they did not wander around the seas as much as the Greeks. Frankly, they are not as interesting. Amun and his wife ruled the winds much as Aeolus was to the Greeks. Henkhisesui took care of the east winds; however, there is limited record about him. Hutchai (that I thought was some kind of mini-grill to fry hamburgers) ran west winds. Qebui, pictured as a ram with wings, catered to the north winds. Shebui, God of the south winds doesn't even have a Wikipedia page. So much for the Egyptians.

Being married to a native Finn, I was fortunate to read a couple of versions of the Kalevala, the mythic epic of early Finland that rivals the Odyssey and was so influential on Henry Wadsworth Longfellow that he adapted the meter of the Kalevala for his poem *Hiawatha*.

Ilmarinen, the blacksmith, used brass, iron, silver, gold, and copper to forge the wonderful Sampo (which, unfortunately, is an entity unknown). Vainamoinen, the demigod, was captured by an old hag, Louhi, an enchantress from Puhjola, promised that if he made her the Sampo, she would ensure him safe passage home. Vainamoinen knew that Ilmarinen could make a Sampo. Ilmarinen got so mad when he was making the Sampo that he called up a massive storm that blew for three days. That's why the Finns connect winds with their legendary craftsman. Well, the rest of the story is long and tedious; but, the Sampo was made and all sorts of adventures happened to poor old Vainamoinen.

While the Kalevala is interesting mythology, it came down thorough the age as oral poems that ultimately were collected and edited by Elias Lonnrot. Not only was Longfellow impacted by the story, elements of the story are seen in FRANKENSTEIN and the LORD OF THE RINGS.

The Finns also have Tuuletar who is the goddess of the wind. While she is not in the Kalevala, most Finns recognize her. Part of the reason for this may be that the Finns moved quickly from their pagan religions to

Lutheranism with a mere nod to the Catholic faith in a short period of time in the 1500's. One excellent example of this is my wife's family have belonged to the same Lutheran congregation since 1550 (we have the records!) and Martin Luther was still preaching in those days.

The Sami are those people who raise reindeer North of the Arctic Circle and freely roam across Norway, Sweden, Finland, and Russia wearing very colorful, albeit warm, clothes. Sami literature is virtually extinct if it ever was significant; however, they did have two gods: Bieggolmai and Bigkegaellies. These are the unpredictable god of summer winds and winter winds respectively.

One of the greatest civilizations to sail the sea and expand thousands of miles before the Europeans even left sight of land were the Proto-Polynesians. The god Maui is an element of New Zealand, Tonga, Tahiti, Hawaii, and Samoa. The fact that this mythical entity is common across the Pacific is evidence of the great travels the early people attempted.

Linguists note an incredible correlation among all the Pacific peoples, and it is the scholars of anthropology and linguistics that show how these people read waves, birds, and the stars to migrate and settle over thousands of miles. Some dates indicate that the earliest Proto-Polynesians were probably from the Chinese coast. Ironically, as China developed as a civilization, the people became deeply entrenched in the region and were not among the explorers. Just why one group left and the later people stayed firmly on land is an interesting question.

Maui is a mischievous character that was never really seen as a god, but more of a folk hero similar to Paul Bunyan. One New Zealand legend is that Maui's brothers would not go fishing with him nor tell him where the fish were biting, so Maui simply made an enchanted flaxen line and made a hook from an old jawbone that had been given to him by his grandmother. The next day, in front of his brothers, he landed a fish so huge it became New Zealand.

Maui's grandmother lived in a cave inside a burning mountain. She gave one of her burning fingernails to her grandson so he could bring fire to his people. Silly Maui quenched each fingernail that she gave him. So enraged with this act of stupidity, Grandma enflamed her grandson who was saved when he called upon a storm god to send a thunderstorm to quench him.

In sundry groups in the Pacific, Maui so loved birds that he created them with colorful songs and bright colors. In another tale, he creates Hawaii. In Tonga, he created the land in a similar story to the New Zealand myth. In the final analysis, Maui may not be revered as a god, per se, but he remains a colorful folk hero.

When one examines the sundry gods of early cultures, it is understandable that they would see gods controlling environmental aspects of life. The Phoenicians, great sea traders all over the Mediterranean, interestingly, had a religion that was greatly influenced by Egypt, the Hebrews, and other neighboring civilizations but they did not honor any specific god of the winds. From Moses to Jesus, these sailors plied the waters but had no god for the most important element of their lives. Strange.

Modern Christian sailors have no gods of winds that they ritually honor. Nevertheless, the Catholic Church, from which all-other Christian denominations evolve, do have Patron Saints to whom they proffer devotion for intercessions with God. Specifically, there is no patron for the winds. St. Medard, a French bishop, has a legend that whatever the weather is like on his feast day, June 8, it will remain that way for 40 days. This story is quite similar to the Church of England's St. Swithun. Note, both are weather related saints but not oriented to the wind alone.

Summers in Iowa tend to be hot, humid, and without any semblance of a breeze. It is the bane of all midwestern sailors. Oh, that we could simply sacrifice a cold beer to appease the god of wind or engulf buckets of shrimp to honor such a deity. Maybe those people of yore had the right idea.

NINE

THE MAGIC OF SAILING

Ah, the magic of sailing is something that is indescribable to the lubber, unfathomable to the uninitiated, and irrational to the cognitive oriented; but it is there. Existential thinkers posit the problem "To be or not to be, that is the question". Magic just is. It exists. Period. There is no explanation for it, no logical rationale to comprehend. I am not talking about David Copperfield kind of magic that is illusion, trick, and misguidance. I am talking about the real stuff. I am talking about the recognizable but totally illogical, incomprehensible, immeasurable stuff that exists.

I learned about magic very, very early in my fledgling year of sailing. Discovery learning taught me several canons of the magical waters. Each season Magical Laws are ascertained. Not unlike our knowledge of space where each additional telescopic photo and fresh extra-planetary satellite proffers greater knowledge, sailing seasons provide us with more understanding of the laws of magic

A. The Primary Laws of Magical Disappearance

<u>1. The Disappearance of Tools</u>.

Another writer noted that every time he started a new project around the boat, a tool disappeared: a ratchet, pliers, and a saw. It was not only consistent over time; it was common among all sailors with whom he shared his learning

A. The Law of Need (corollary to Law #1.)

1- I totally concur but add this slight variation or addendum: the loss is proportional to the need at that time. If you have everything in place for that last bolt to finalize the project, the bolt will disappear. If you have the plan in hand; all the boards ready, measured, and marked; the pieces all clamped, then the saw will disappear. My encounter with this magic came when I needed to move my boat immediately to a new anchorage. My new (read that "brand spanking new, straight from the store, still in the package, receipt in the pocket" new) anchor that had held my boat with incredible firmness literally disappeared from the end of the rode. I hauled up the rope which was heavy from the weight of the anchor right up to the side of the boat only to pull the end of the line out with the anchor gone, gone, gone. Furthermore, this anchor was attached with the best of the U.S. Navy's Boot Camp marline spike expert knot: an anchor knot with a double half hitch on a bowline on a bight. Moby Dick couldn't get away from that knot. Three honest-to-God Chief Bo' sun Mates couldn't untie that thing.

1 – B. The Law of Value (second corollary to Law #1.)

Right along with the law of need comes value: the more valuable the item, the faster it will disappear. How expensive is your GPS toy? If it is really good and expensive, the chances of it quickly evaporating into the ethers are very high. The $ 2 compass from Wal-Mart will somehow float up from the TITANIC, but your GARMIN 459XLM thousand-dollar GPS will fly away as soon as you turn your back on it. I know, I have gone through several. I discovered that even with a small dinghy a good fish finder is a wonderful way of knowing water temperature, depth, speed, etc., as well as showing you the abundance of fish beneath you. These are not particularly inexpensive for us dinghy people. Two have magically disappeared from the bottom of my boat while sailing in gentle breezes on Pleasant Creek Lake in Iowa. Of course, it must be magic since both were tied to some part of the boat. Even a whole mast, boom, and sail can disappear. Once in early April when the ice had left my favorite Iowa lake, I sailed my beautiful Boatex 1200 and magically capsized for no reason at all (in a section of the lake where my other materials had disappeared; I call it the Bermuda Triangle). I righted my boat only to find that boom, mast, and all had magically disappeared. Further proof can be added that the entire Linn County Search and Recovery team could not find any semblance of it after going through many, many air tanks while on the hunt. I know, I dived on the site too.

Answer: magic.

B. The Primary Laws of Magical Waters

Anything that is considered a body of water is, by definition, magic. Consider that water drains in clockwise spirals in one hemisphere and counter clockwise in the other. Water turns to ice and ice floats. As a former academic dean, I have tolerated a plethora of lectures replete with diagrams, statistics, and mathematical formulas. From this I have deduced that:

a) $H2O$ is water,

b) $E=MC2$

c) K9P is what my dog leaves on my deck.

<u>B 1. The Law of Weird Waters.</u>

As just written, the Bermuda triangle (Iowa's version of the Bermuda Triangle) is a spot half way across the lake between the handicapped fishing dock (I don't know if the dock is for handicapped people or just handicapped fishermen) and directly in line with the dam. It is here where all dinghies must overturn. It is also the only spot on the lake that is greater than 25 feet deep. Here it is 65 feet of highly sludgy, dirty, cold, and dark water. Having dived on that spot I can attest that visibility is absolutely zero, a visual equal to Physics absolute zero. Other sailors tell me that such spots are not unusual, especially on lakes with "newbie" sailors.

B 2. The Law of Waves.

The direction of waves has no correlation with wind, current, tides, or Newtonian Physics. Waves in the water are an element of Quantum Mechanics that is beyond human comprehension and is all probably nothing more than a whim of very sick scientists.

B 3. The Law of Color.

The color of water is like a chameleon. One minute it is brown, suddenly it is dark green, or it miraculously becomes light blue. The Pacific Ocean tends to be mud colored near California but somehow changes to florescent blue at Pebble Beach, and it becomes a brilliant blue at Hawaii but a light blue inside the reef at Guam. The Atlantic Ocean is never blue. Ever. The Gulf of Mexico's color is unknown. Water is far beneath the thick layer of oil.

As for all the prosaic and terminally boring attempt to understand water, the physicists are all crazier than loons. All of it can be easily explained: Its Magic.

C. The Primary Laws of the Wind

C 1. The Law of Unpredictability.

It is totally impossible for a sailor to understand the wind. If the breeze at your residence is gale force, the Law of Wind says that the lake will be quieter than bath water. If you happen to step outside to see nary a leaf bobbing and you decide to go to the lake to clean the boat or whatever and you will find an unnamed hurricane blowing steadily.

C 1.-A. Corollary to Law C. The Law of Important Visitors.

When you have friends on your little craft and you are trying to impress them with your nautical skills, the lake will have great and splendid breezes all over its entire surface EXCEPT wherever you happen to be. That spot will be stiller than a dead man's breath

C1-B. Second Corollary to Law C The Law of Position.

A second corollary is that if you are somewhat a neophyte sailor, the lake will be extraordinarily moderate in winds EXCEPT where you are. That specific place will have white caps, rouge waves, and a frequency to amplitude correlation that would flip an aircraft carrier

C 1.-C Third Corollary to Law C The Law of Observers.

A third corollary is that the probability of the second corollary is perfectly correlated to how many people are watching you or how much you want to impress the people in your boat. If you are single and male with a gorgeous, bodacious Swedish blonde, bikini clad Victoria's Secret model in the boat sailing on a park pond, the chances of a Tsunami the size of the Sears Tower hitting you are precisely 100%.

A myriad of other nautical laws exists, some of which I shall ponder in future editions of this epistle; however, I propose that other seafaring philosophers add their perspectives as well. To understand water, we must hang together. Sailors must hold on to each other or Neptune will devour us all just for the hell of it.

TEN

POKE ABOUT

Small Craft Advisor contains articles and photos of newly launched boats of exquisite beauty, superb craftsmanship, and precise construction that whet my appetite for a wooden boat hewn from exotic lumber, nurtured with diligence, and birthed in my backyard with patience and deliberate care. Two years ago, I made the leap after SCA magazine seized my cerebral cortex and forced the limbic system to excrete gallons of hormones and behavioral chemicals resulting in an obsessive-compulsive drive unstoppable until the completion of a boat.

Unfortunately, this story does not culminate with photos of a beautiful boat making sailors and lubbers alike drool. Worse, this is not the kind of article usually found on the pages of such a quality magazine. The editors of **Mad Magazine** would reject this out of kindness to humanity. This written experience will probably exude tears of sadness over a waste of good wood, nausea over the lack of knowledge, and maybe even frustration about the stupidity exhibited. I blame the school counselors.

Back in the early 60s, the Sputnik Crisis aroused huge indignation that America had allowed the Soviet Union to launch an artificial satellite into space before we could develop a technology of similar ilk. The requisite prescription was to identify highly intelligent students and herd them into the sciences while driving the dolts and sloths into "shop" classes. I was informed that I would be among those who piloted rockets to Mars or solved the contradictions existing between Newtonian and Quantum mechanics. I was barred from the school's basement housing the Industrial Arts department. God and Congress ordained me to mix two clear liquids resulting in a purple precipitate or to solve calculus equations. Calluses were for mere mortals.

Many decades later I found myself shaking with Obsessive-Compulsive desires to build a boat. For the record, I left the world of chemistry and pharmaceuticals for a degree in history and graduate degrees in psychology. Interestingly, I never have been required to parse a Latin phrase or solve a quadratic equation; however, as a home owner I find myself hiring people to fix leaky faucets, cut firewood, or operate a toilet plunger. In the Navy I was tested about what kind of wrench should be used on various types of problems. I did not know that there were different kinds of wrenches. The military put me behind a desk and told me not to cause any trouble or get in anyone's way.

Mississippi Bob Brown, a renowned boat builder and designer of small craft, teased me unmercifully about my ignorance of tools and building design. He candidly says, "No one is THAT stupid." Evidently, I am.

Just to prove the old Coast Guard veteran and lockmaster wrong, I purchased plans for a floating object called a Poke About that supposedly is the easiest thing in the world to build. The directions said from acquisition of lumber to floating in the lake would take a full weekend. I started the first week of June. It took five months of steady, mind-numbing work in 90-degree temperatures.

Actually, I had to make a modest pre-building operation by going to Home Depot and buying all sorts of tools: drill, sander, saw, epoxy, pliers, screwdrivers, nails, and a thing called a planer. A trip to a lumberyard produced a couple of 4x8 pieces of plywood, some 2x4s, some screws of sundry sizes, and some directions on how to use epoxy. The plywood flew off the car at the first corner. I slept though knot-tying (marlinspike?) classes in boot camp.

The *Poke About* is a very cool little boat. It is one of those take-apart things where the bow end fits nicely in the stern when travelling. Once at the water the two ends are bolted together and away you go paddling like crazy. The 34-page instructions were complete with photographs and ideas for extending it to a two-person boat or adding a small electric motor. It even had ideas about additional floatation for large people. I did not read the directions but I did examine the pictures closely.

With missionary zeal I commenced sawing and hacking. The directions I had purchased said something about a board with a 17-degree slant lengthwise, an end cut at 28 degrees while the other end was to be at 73 degrees. After sawing a couple of 2x4s it dawned on me that it was important to have the fatter end at the 17 degrees rather than the other end. I only made that mistake about four times. Several trips to the lumberyard later I did not have to worry about hauling wood; they kindly delivered.

As grumpy old men are wont to say, they just don't make tools like they used to. First, my circular saw caught on fire and scared the heck out of my wife when she saw flames and smoke emitting from my saw. I continued to work intuiting that as long as the saw blade continued to cut, so should I. Second, the high-quality sander featuring the name of a respected company suddenly made noises uncommon for woodworking utensils. Trying to figure what was going on, I started and stopped it several times until little ball bearings and springs were ejected at high velocity. Third, the saber saw, a replacement for my father's that once shot sparks across the garage and blew out the circuit panel, worked well but the blades kept snapping off at inappropriate times.

The hull of this boat is extraordinarily simple: a trapezoid 36 inches on one side and 24 inches on the other. The forward bottom deck is 24 inches tapered to 17 inches. For each of these two floors one attaches four bulkheads. When completed the two boxes are bolted together to make the boat. When apart, the forward compartment fits nicely into the rear. Simple, or so I thought.

When measuring out the floor panels I took extreme care to ensure proper measurements. Unfortunately. I evidently did not find the precise center of the plywood board so that when I cut my tapered sides one was about 1/2 inch longer than the other. Clearly this indicated that the front would not fit the back unless that too was cut with a skewer. This required another trip to the lumberyard. I shall not mention that I failed to note the page that showed how to get as many wood pieces from a single piece of plywood; nor shall I mention that I cut the front piece twice rather the one for the rear. Plywood is plentiful and I never admit mistakes.

The entire project was designed for stitch-and-glue joinery but I had never attempted this technique so the old-fashioned nail-the-plywood to a 2x2 glued to the bottom of the boat. The concept of nails and screws offer more confidence than an experimental trick. Yet again accurate measurement failed and the wood piece glued to the bottom was a bit too short thus at the junction of the sides to the bulkhead in the middle was without any semblance of connection. This did not seem a problem for my nimble mind since I was going to use fiberglass and epoxy on the seams.

The forward module was another box except for the gentle curve of the bottom rising to meet the bow. I had geometry in 1963. My knowledge of curves is microscopic, and my comprehension of curve drawing is non-existent. I tried sundry homemade protractors (string and chalk) but found nothing that started gradually and tightened sharply toward the end. Even freehand attempts did not achieve much functionality or exquisiteness. The solution came in a moment of frustration and anger when I just sawed off the bottom where the curve should have commenced and merely slanted it to the bow.

The genius who designed this petite craft called this "fun, unique, and easy to build". Obviously, he never met a technological and industrial disaster of my ability. He stated," it's very important that you ensure the Forward Module is aligned properly, before applying the Base Panel, check by the A-B and C-D measurement method." My small little compartment was skewed about 1 inch indicating that the front of the section and the rear of the section were not parallel. See my above comment about plywood being easily obtained. I no longer used the word "cheap" in discussions of my boat building.

This supposedly weekend adventure was entering its fifth month of trial and error when it was decided to start the easy glassing of the seams. An entirely too large a roll of fiberglass tape arrived from West Marine or Fisheries Supply. I made a table from badly cut plywood and some uneven sawhorses. Intuitively I reasoned that this process would be quick, easy, and would solve my many joinery concerns. 1 quart of epoxy, 1 little tube of hardener, a plastic cup, and a shoddy foam brush were placed with much alacrity upon my table. A nicely measured length of tape was slathered with epoxy and applied with enthusiasm and gentle care.

As a person with a doctorate in educational psychology with a specialization in learning, I know and comprehend sundry methods of knowledge acquisition, and I grasp that each person's most effective and efficient processes for said acquisition are different. Personally, I find that reading directions is significantly less successful than hands-on experiential education. With this in mind I learned several additional concepts including:

- Epoxy hardens fairly quickly

- Foam brushes fall off the handle easily

- Slathered fiberglass tape can slide with the least touch

- Fiberglass tends to leave a crease and a void at corners

- Epoxy makes a magnificent mess when spilled on garage floors, tables, or sidewalks.

My experiential learning experience altered my perception so that my boat required additional epoxy after a lengthy and tedious sanding of drips, runs, and errors (apologies to Johnny Bench). My new orbital sander was constantly resurfaced with various grits of sandpaper that produced not inconsiderable white dust clouds that clogged all aural and nasal orifices to the point of virtual asphyxiation. Ace Hardware clerks greeted me with open arms while enriching my basket with facemasks and goggles. My wife said something to the effect that "By God you aren't coming into MY house covered with all that dust." At least I made the Ace Hardware people happy.

After additional touching up of nooks and crannies but prior to actual beautification of my boat, I was ready for a trial run. My wife scanned the insurance policies and decided she had best attend this operation for fear of my drowning and leaving her penniless. We quietly slipped down to a rarely used dock along the Cedar River and waited until we were certain that no one would see us, especially if the thing sank like a rock. I bolted the two modules together, and launched it gently into the water. No sooner than the plywood touch water than up pulls a truck with a monstrous pit-bull hanging out the window and drooling down the door. My frustration in having a strange observer fulminated to full seething when out popped not a stranger but my brother of great talents and a firm belief that all the family intelligence was reserved for him instead of being divided equally between us. Laughing uproariously and with jabbing comments about ugliness at a public nature reserve, he whipped out his camera to record this initial trial run for posterity, if not for the funeral obituary.

I clambered in my wee craft and commenced paddling with a kayak paddle. It did not take a Ph.D. to quickly observe that this entity of a vessel leaked like a kitchen colander. Stroking for my life I managed to get the Poke About from the dock to the landing without swamping. Inspection noted that all the corners were leaky. Surprisingly my brother did not smirk but merely suggested additional epoxy, lots of epoxy. Worse, I had added two boxes of Styrofoam for additional floatation but this was too much and I was floating in about an inch of water being blown around by the slightest of breezes. I added 50 pounds of lead and sawed off the extra floatation.

After sanding off all the wrinkles and air pockets I indeed blanketed the craft with about a quart of epoxy. Skipping to page 15 in the direction manual I read that coating the interior with

Thompson's Water Seal was essential. I reasoned logically that the exterior is as important as the interior it too should be covered. Unfortunately, I did not read that painting should precede this endeavor, and when I slapped on water-based paint it literally slid off the boat. A fine oil-based paint was painstakingly applied which seemed to work.

The following summer (remember it was supposed to be built over a weekend), I discovered even more leaks and the paint needed a total re-do. Again, Ace hardware enjoyed profits from my project boat. And yet again I forgot to check whether it was water based or oil-based paints so I got to do this job a couple of times. In the meantime, my brother simply gave me his kayak. But I was darned if I couldn't complete this "weekend" task.

The boat was placed on stands, filled with water, thoroughly checked for leaks, and was cleared for future use. I will use my brother's paddle since I can't afford one. The boat was named after my favorite Florida bar, **Sea Hag**, to reflect the fact that this thing is one ugly duckling. The next time I will buy a kit. My wife agrees.

ELEVEN

MY WIFE HATES SAILING, THANK GOD

This morning I was exiting the shower when I realized that my body wash was Hawaiian Garden (cocoanut and hibiscus), my shampoo was green tea and "organic" aloe, my conditioner was lilac, the hand soap was vanilla and mint, and my deodorant was "Tahiti" which was some sort of tropical floral scent. Heck, I smelled like some sort of Island drink served in a pineapple with an umbrella. According to Blue Collar comic and wit, Jeff Foxworthy, I am either Gay or I am married.

I confess to the latter. For 40 years Ms. Frozen Finland and I have been in happy bliss, and she reminds me how wonderfully lucky and happy I am…each and every day. Unceasingly. My occasional escape, excuse me, time away from my happy existence, is to go sailing. Ms. I-am-Nordic-not-Scandinavian, dislikes man-made lakes, rivers, wind, heeling, lines and things that go bight, docks, dampness, excessive sun, uncomfortable cushions, PFDs, and the wasted time watching her dopey husband raise a mast and set the sails. For this, I am eternally grateful.

Here's how I see it: God really did not intend for women to be on sailing boats. Oh sure, the periodic boat with the bikini clad blonde sunning herself on the bow is certainly one of the charms of boating. And the female who cooks the meals at Messabouts is accepted. But on board, no way.

If Ms. Suomen Silta herself were into this boating recreation, I would experience life as no self-respecting Man Jack could imagine. The boat would be painted in beige or a pastel blue with appropriate trim in chromic symmetry, perhaps a turquoise. The bright work would be highly polished and constantly dusted. Seating would be oversized cushions in contrasting colors to the hull and in a floral print designed by Marimekko. The tiller would be of Finnish spruce or Nordic birch enveloped by nautical knots and marlinspike. Shoes would be taken off before boarding.

Miss Sauna would have one installed on the boat even if it was a dinghy. All Finnish people have a sauna close at hand. My one and only time aboard a saltwater boat built in Finland did indeed have a sauna in place of a berth.

Beer would be banned from the boat. White wine would be the adult beverage of choice (she is partial to Iowa Chablis or Chardonnay but occasionally a California Riesling would suffice. If spaghetti is served, a quiet Chianti is unopposed. However, all glasses would be Iittala glassware designed by Tapio Wirkkala and imported directly from Stockman's in Helsinki.

All communications equipment would be, by mandate, Nokia. For that matter, our foulies and boots would be Nokia also. For those who don't know it, Nokia started as a rubber boot company and accidently developed cell phones.

The boat itself must never, ever heel; be attacked by mosquitoes, lack air conditioning (she can't handle humidity), and be deficient in full sanitary equipment including a pulsating shower and large sink. Cooking would be accomplished by the full-sized stove and oven under the microwave and next to the Frigidaire with freezer. The berthing spaces would be quilted in distinct colors complete with a Serta mattress and a nautically carved, polished teak headboard. Pillows would be Nordic Goose down and stuffed to a firmness unsurpassed in mere American department stores. The figurehead, that all boats must have, would be a moose head or at least antlers -- not that she'd be concerned about a foul anchor rode, tangled mooring lines, or stuck bumper.

Thus, I get on my knees to proffer thanks and offerings to the Great God Neptune that my wife dislikes boats. I feel a necessity to give praise by consuming quantities of ale and lager at dockside bars with indigent water rats while conversing about sail repair and how best to paint the decks. We all have that look of manly men who have escaped the clutches of spouses who are fuming about yard mowing and screen door patching while we congregate among fellow sailors enjoying the pleasure of our company. Our boats match our personalities: in need of repair, paint, cleaning, and TLC. But we, God's Chosen Few, continue to tinker, purchase, and sail to our hearts content in eternal gratitude that our wives hate boats.

TWELVE

NAUTICAL GRIEF

Many years ago, I studied death and dying under the renowned Dr. Elizabeth Kubler-Ross at Mayo Clinic. Among the many things I learned was that there are several kinds of grief such as simple grief (loss of a loved one) and complex grief (loss of a pet or something prized). I am suffering the latter.

It is complex because not only is the person for whom I grieve someone I never knew or ever met. That person, in fact, is imaginary! You see, I just finished the 20th and last book of the Patrick O'Brian series, and now I grieve that I shall no longer sail the ships and seas with Captain Jack Aubrey and his host of friends and shipmates.

The loss of Aubrey and his surgeon friend, Stephen Maturin, mean that the voyages around the Horn, the battles with the accursed French, the futile internecine wars within the Admiralty, and the essence of great ship handling are to disappear. Among those lost are the perpetually faithful but simple Padeen, the ever-competent Bondon, the chronically complaining Killick, the loyal Captain Pullings, and a host of other souls who crewed **Surprise** and other ships under the command of Lucky Jack.

Under the good Captain, I learned about brigs, and barks, and xebecs. I enjoyed knowing that the dreaded Spanish, **Cacafeugo**, was named humorously in Spanish and, translated literally, means "Shit-Fire": great joke from O'Brian. The crew taught me about staysails, royals, skysails, courses, and topsails, and what to fly in hurricanes or what to do in irons. I learned the Articles of War and how to brew arrack. They taught a burgeoning nautical vocabulary of tall ships. My knowledge swelled and my interest in ships blossomed. But now they are gone.

Yes, I realize that there remains Hornblower, Frost, Ramage, and a plethora of others. Still, I long for one more time to lean against the taffrail of the **Surprise** watching the topmen reefing a course or witnessing the massive spread while running before the wind. I wish for yet another lecture on the ligature of a split artery or the evolution of tropical ants. Ah yes, I grieve.

THIRTEEN

EXPERIENTIAL LEARNING

I have a doctorate in educational psychology and have long studied the sundry processes of learning and the incredible variances in learning styles. Some of us learn by reading, some by listening, some by observation, and some seemingly by osmosis. The one methodology spewed forth by many scholars who obviously never sailed a boat in their lives, is experiential learning. These lubbers subscribe to the theory that one learns best by active, hands-on, participation in the activity.

Bob Bitchin, the irreverent publisher of *LATITUDES AND ATTITUDES*, once wrote, "Good judgment comes from experience. Experience comes from Bad Judgment". I think he hates experiential learning as much as me. Trust me I have had more than my fair share of this method of sailing education.

Those of you who have managed not to gag on my previous vexations know of my deep and personal repulsion of all things rope. Now I know that all you old salts and sea dogs are sniveling about someone designating shrouds, stays, rode, and halyards as ropes. Sorry folks, but that is what it is, dammit. I have hurled a plethora of rope over the side attempting to anchor unattached bitter ends. I have lost mounds of coils of rope when turning turtle in deep water. I have indeed capsized with sundry strands of the stuff wrapping around my ankles and/ or breaking the mast in foul weather. I truly hate all things hemp (except smoking it as a frat rat at Upper Iowa University).

Only hoses rank close in the category of disdain. Hoses manage to curl in knots as you pump the bilge creating an environment where only a couple of finger lacerations and three or four contusions and abrasions are resulting. All hoses, whether gas lines or pump or other type are incredibly inflexible at the moment you require flexibility or flexible when you need rigidity. My dislike of all hoses comes from experiential learning. I did, however, invest in Johnson and Johnson to make fiduciary gain from my requisite Band Aids.

Experientially I have learned that standing up in a small dinghy is unwise. Unfortunately, one learns from one's mistakes, and a wise one learns from other's mistake. I, however, have needed several experiences to learn this particular lesson. Worse, my pocket book has been the just punishment for learning about properly securing a freestanding mast. Tip over and mast, boom, and mainsail go into the depths. With the able assistance of the Linn County Search and Recovery team we made a series of cold-water dives in November and still could not recover the items. The following spring a friend did recover the items and this was a lesson learned. Yeah, learned until the next sail when I repeated the whole thing all over again. OK, I am a slow, slow learner. Ph.D. or not, I learn slowly, especially experientially.

Iowa is hardly the sailboat center of the universe. My first dinghy was purchased in Canada from the esteemed Roger Poole whose father developed the Boatex line. Yet again I learned the hard way that trying to transfer a boat from the Canadian city of Toronto to the wilderness of Iowa is impossible. Evidently, the Border Patrol of the Homeland Security department (am I the only one who finds the name Homeland Security slightly reminiscent of Nazi Germany?) decided that anything nautical was probably a weapon of mass destruction. Six months of pain, on the new trailer I discovered that the guide bunks were too narrow and the boat simply did not fit. No problem: simply call the Fickle Finn and have her return. But my phone was also in her car. I forced the boat to about a 45-degree angle on the trailer, tied it down with the shrouds, and very, very slowly drove the 15 miles home. This is another example of experiential learning that I will never, ever share with my friend Mississippi Bob who already acknowledges that he can see no smidgen of learning gained during my 12 weeks of Navy Boot Camp. He simply nodded knowingly when he heard I was assigned to an Army Post after my initial Navy training.

A proud agnostic who has a bumper sticker saying, "Agnostic: you don't know; neither do I", Mississippi Bob brings out rosary beads, a yarmulke, incense, St. Christopher medals, and lights candles to the Blessed Virgin when he knows that I am about to sail. He also warns his colleagues at the Coast Guard.

Well, I have adjusted the bunks and am about ready to face the Minnesota Messabout folks. My ready excuse to my experiential learning is that I am old, I am an eccentric Ph.D., and I am from Iowa. Still, wouldn't it have been easier to take a class or something??!

FOURTEEN

GODS OF THE SEA AND WATER

Those of us who light candles, finger beads, and wear prayer shawls to a plethora of Gods of Water and Sea who seemingly demand significant catering to and worship sacrifices. I down a beer or two at the Tic Toc Tap or Schuey's as ceremonial rites of worship thanking the many gods for my not drowning. When I am on the pontoon, I restrict my on-board intake to Cokes or Mountain Dew and granola bars while facing forward with head religiously bowed.

No god is more famous than that old Greek, Poseidon, son of Cronus and Rhea, and a brother to Zeus. He invented the horse. What that has to do with sailing is beyond me but so is Quantum Mechanics. He is a moody guy who never quite over his father swallowing him as a baby. He was a middle child and has behaved like one for a long, long time. He was angered when Athens refused his offering of a salt pool by the temple and those unfortunate citizens accepted the olive tree from Athena instead. When truly irate, he causes earthquakes and floods. While he may not be a nice guy, you have to watch out and not aggravate him.

Hydros is the grandfather of Poseidon and has been around since the beginning of time. He is so old that he did not have any parents, but he did sire Cronus. He gave his name to water. Because of him we have hydroelectric dams and hydraulics.

Ceto is a malevolent god of sea monsters. She sired children with her brother that was something of a No-No even on Mount Olympus. Of course, her kids were all terrifying sea monsters, dragons, and sharks. She cackles with glee when chaos erupts on the high seas. Scuba divers need pay attention to her. On the other hand, the first time I saw a shark while scuba diving in Cozumel, it had seen so many, many divers daily it posed for photos, signed autographs, and swam around nicely.

Glaucus is somewhat of a nicer god. He is the god of fishermen and of prophecy. I have, unfortunately, failed in showing him enough respect, and I am, therefore, the world's worst fisherman with proof to show for it. I spent an entire day in the Dismal Swamp trying to untangle my ball of line because I did not know how to use an open-faced spinning reel. And when I was fishing in Finland with my then 12-year-old son, all I caught was a duck. Glaucus, clearly, was unappeased.

Oceanus is another nice guy and good son. I think of him sitting on the beach working on his tan, sipping cold ambrosia, ogling the girls in thongs, and cogitating about the lobster he will have for dinner. He is the brother to Zeus, Hades, and Poseidon but he refused to assist them in the ouster of their father as head dude of Mount Olympus. His kids are nymphs, springs, and fountains. He is the God of Fresh Water.

The Egyptians had their own gods of water such as Anuket, daughter of Ra, who also is the goddess of childbirth. The relationship between the Nile River and childbirth is interesting. Possibly because children are formed in a sack of water or because the flooding of the river gives water to the soil so it can be farmed, Anuket was proclaimed a goddess. She is a bit temperamental and needy, wanting others to carry her luggage. Like a lot of women, she loves gold and the old Egyptians hurled gold into the river to keep her happy. Pharaohs were no bottle babies; they were suckled by good old Anuket.

Tefnut is the goddess of rain. Because the resources of Egypt are so precarious, this is one goddess to keep happy. Incest keeps a family together. She married her twin brother, Shu, and had two kids: Geb and Nut. If for no other reason, I love her because of the names of her children. She had the head of a lion and the body of a woman who the priests were supposed to apply sacred oils. Interesting gal but not one to bring home to mother!

Not far away from Egypt lies India, a subcontinent that is replete with cultures and languages and religion that no one book could capture its complexity. Hinduism does permeate much of the area, and it too has gods and goddesses for the sea and waters.

One of my favorites is Ganga who is a lovely lady who is noted for mercy, health, cleansing, and protection. One little drop of water from the Ganges will cure you of all your problems and (better yet) forgives you for your past indiscretions. She also controls Makara, a sea monster who likes to mess with sailors on the seas.

King Varna is the oldest of the Vedic gods, and he created the world. Being the creator of all, he controls everything especially endeavors dealing with water. Unlike Ganga, he demands justice – swift and stern. He will forgive if you pray for it and repent. He is portrayed as having 1,000 eyes and can detect all sinners.

The Chinese, not known for drifting too far out to sea, have their own goddess of the sea. Interestingly, linguists and anthropologists have examined the sundry languages of the Pacific Islands and easily understood that from Guam to Hawaii, and Micronesia to Polynesia that the languages are remarkably similar to each other and to ancient China. Evidently, the Chinese took off on great explorations but later gave up that idea and decided to stay home and make pre-historic computer chips or something.

Anyway, Mazu was born human but achieved divinity after becoming a prodigy of Buddhist and Daoist mysteries. She can prophesize bad weather and warns sailors of bad seas. She also rescues sailors dumped overboard.

Afro-Caribbean culture has their own goddess of the water, Mami Wata, a mermaid that has been a fixture of the Caribbean and South American for over 500 years. Oddly, she is also associated with finances, and if you manage to antagonize her, she will simply destroy your fiscal resources. Mami Wata is an admixture of African religions, Christianity, and Hinduism. We better pay attention to her since she crosses several religions. You just have to cover all your possibilities.

Being an old Irishman and a descendent of folks from County Cork, I pay attention to the old Celtic gods and goddesses of the sea. Boann is the goddess of the river Boyne, duh. Her name means "white cow". She was married to Elcmar but got pregnant by the Dagda, an important god in charge of strength, courage, water, and virility. The Dagda realizes that this will be something of an issue so he simply makes the sun stand still and masking the pregnancy from Elcmar. In one tale she goes to a well to cleanse herself but drowns. In another tale, her little lap dog is washed out to sea and dies but the canine body became the rocks *Cnoc Dabilla*, or Hill of Dabilla.

The Norse, whose Leif Erickson may have been among the first Europeans to discover North America, naturally had a couple a gods. Njord, father of Freyr and Freyja, controlled the wind and the sea. As a Vanir god (as opposed to an Aegir god), he is associated with fertility, wealth, and commerce. He, obviously, was an early capitalist since making money is associated with getting the girls.

Aegir is an older deity in the Norse pantheon and his name means water. The old Vikings feared him and offered sacrifices to avoid shipwreck.

Anyone who has taken a linguistics class knows that languages travel and they get altered a little bit along the way. Polynesian and Māori cultures have a god named Tangaroa or Kanaloa (you can see the similarities). He controls the tides and is the god for sailors. In Samoa, this god is considered the Chief God and creator of all things.

In the final analysis, all cultures have worried about traveling on the water or fearing the destructive havoc rendered by waters. Having a god to pray to, sacrifice to, and plead to is an essential element of society that does voyage on water. The Biblical quote that this evokes is simply:

> They that go down to the sea in ships,
> And do business in Great Waters,
> They shall see the works of the Lord
> And His wonders of the deep.

Compliments of:

Jana Louise Smit, "Water Gods and Sea Gods From Around the World", History Cooperative, April 28, 2020, https://historycooperative.org/water-gods-gods-of-the-sea/. Accessed May 20, 2022

Nina Jay, "Water Gods in Different Cultures and Mythologies" https://symbolsage.com/water-gods-list/. Accessed May 26, 2022.

FIFTEEN

I LOVE SMALL BOATS

During a meeting on small boat safety, the instructor asked the simple question, "Who is planning for your next boat?". Everyone raised their hands, and each was thinking about a bigger boat. I too have longingly eyed the yachts, the longer and nicer boats. I too have yearned for a little more cockpit room or an additional sized cabin or a wee bit of greater storage space; however, this came smashing on the shoals of reality.

Let us not cogitate a single moment upon the creeping up of old age nor grimace at the sound of creaking knees. Let us not note the aches and pains that arise with us each dawn (or 9:00 am for me). Let us focus, indeed, upon the withering realization of our own ignorance or at least our unwillingness to desire new learning.

SAIL magazine, that slick rag redolent with provocative photos of yachts with spinnakers flying, guests smiling with joyous rapture while holding their wine glasses and staring over a banquet of lobster or shrimp, bikinis galore, tanned sailors in splendid attire, and an azure sea splitting like Moses' waters cleft by the bow of a sleek vessel brought me to a stunning halt in daydreaming. If that did not stem my fantasies, other magazines did.

Before you even think about a craft worthy of circumnavigation or a quick vacation to Bermuda, you have to spend endless weeks searching for the perfect boat. It must be surveyed, repaired, and customized to fit you needs and whims. A lovely older 2006 Oceanis 523 can be your baby for a mere $250,000 or a 2005 Leopard 47 for $289,000. Hey, maybe you would rather have a catamaran with four staterooms and four heads. A nice little Catana 47 will only set you back about $800,000. Pocket change for us mortals.

Being a traditionalist, you want a single hull cruiser. Then you have to know whether you want a fin keel, a full keel, wing keel, bulb keel, or bilge keels. A ketch is beautiful, a sloop looks speedy, and schooners are complicated. It does not make any difference. Have it delivered immediately by Adam Cort. Your slip expense is irrelevant.

But the expenditures creep silently through the hawse pipe. That slick sailing journal that is a requisite reading for all sailors shows some the equipment any imbecile on the water must have. You will experience foul weather, and it is essential for you to possess foulies that include: pants, jacket, hat, socks, boots, and gloves. Heavy seas will necessitate a myriad of sails, lines that can be controlled from the cockpit, sea anchors, and a darn good bilge pump. In case all else fails you need an EPIRB, a couple of radios - at least one of which must be a handheld model, a life raft that can handle a half dozen guests, and flare guns, mirrors, Life vests, whistles, horns, immersion suits, emergency strobes, first aid kits, radar reflectors, and fire extinguishers.

I am mechanically challenged compliments of Sputnik whose orbit sent the American political entities into paroxysms of trepidation. Congress blamed Ike, the Republicans blamed the Democrats, the Church blamed the devil, and Europe blamed the U.S. It was all quite bewildering to a kid in elementary school. Our wise folk under the Great Dome in Washington decided we had an urgent need for more scientists and schools were ordered to push students into college. It was under this guidance that we who seemed to have some semblance of intelligence were suddenly rammed into math and science classes; but more importantly, we were forbidden to partake in Industrial Arts classes, Art programs, and anything other than higher level math and physics.

By the time I graduated from college (with a degree in history since I was kicked out of Pharmacy College because I did not comprehend Inorganic Chemistry or Calculus), the Viet Nam War was blasting away mightily. I entered the Navy that tested the daylights out of me. On the mechanical section I was presented with a problem and was given four possible wrenches to use. I had no idea that there even were four types of wrenches. I have neither knowledge nor experience with anything other than a hammer.

My plethora of sailing magazines virtually flood readers with DIY information on repair of water-makers, generators, motors, and gears and pullies and stuff. I know a propeller when I see one but I have no clue about an impeller. I did learn that ropes are on a spool and become lines when used. Evidentially this is because of transmogrification.

All I understand about electricity is how to plug-in a lamp. I do know that a battery is in a car and occasionally needs replacement because the car won't run. My sailing friends swoon with ecstatic pleasure discussing deep cycle batteries or whether lead batteries are no longer acceptable on boats. They talk about a gel battery when I thought gel was for keeping my thinning hair in place. One erudite owner haughtily posited the benefits of an Absorbed Glass Mat battery. Someone mentioned parallel versus series wiring. They might as well be speaking Finnish.

After two decades of sailing small boats, I cannot figure out what a Comfort Ratio is. In my little West Wight Potter 15, comfort is a sunny day with a decent breeze and does not require mathematics. Ballast to Displacement ratio can be answered in two words," Who cares!" In fact, my wife constantly barrages me with chronic concern about my "ballast". She does not know anything about length at waterline but she does recognize my beltline.

Now a Mariner 39 looks like a really nice boat about which I dream; but to compare her to a Gulfstar 39 or Pacific Seacraft 40 is a bit like asking me to compare the pulchritude of two gorgeous movie stars. I am pretty sure that I could never even get an autograph from a beautiful starlet, and I am equally sure that I could never sail any of these craft.

Nope, I am sorry but my dreams are simply bubbling imagination. I will raise my mast by myself, launch my somewhat dirty boat, sail solo around a man-made lake at speeds approaching 5 knots. It takes no level of genius to make her go nor does it require any arithmetic. Navigation is easy. You just follow the shoreline, stay in the middle of the lake to avoid the rocks, and you simply turn around when you want to go home.

A small boat does not need a variety of sails. A jib and a mainsail do just fine. Most of my lakeside friends have only two sails. Storm jibs are basic insults at a dockside tavern, spinnakers are old unmarried women, and Genoa is the nuclear power plant in Wisconsin.

Over the years many sailing magazine writers discussed gel cracks that I fail to comprehend since gel cracks are sarcasm about my coiffured hair. West Wight Potter folks claim that gel cracks are rarely an issue with their boats, and a lot of them are old. The boats, not the people.

Blistering remains another concern that does not concern me. I get blisters from sunburn (especially on that certain spot atop my head). They do bother my wife who chronically berates me for lack of hat usage despite heaps of them in the closet. She also says I should utilize lotion or sunscreen. But that stuff makes my hands slippery and I need a firm grasp with such items as the tiller or the lines. I bought several pairs of sailing gloves but they evidently ended up in the box with mittens and scarves.

Nope, you can keep your 36-footer. Living in the state of Iowa, I have no reason to spend the night aboard ship. Tie up and head to the nearest motel, especially one's that serve free breakfast, have comfortable toilets, showers with ample warm water, and electricity. You cannot do that in the middle of the Pacific. The Beneteau sailors can brag, look natty, and discuss their circumnavigation till hell freezes over, but a Super 8 has better beds.

Sometimes the Yacht Club types will think and discuss the complexities, pros and cons, and the methodology of anchoring. Being a scholar of immodest levels and master of insignificant trivia, I know that the word "anchor" comes from the Latin 'ancora' that actually comes from the Greek 'auncura'; however, do not ask me about types because they simply are not an issue with small boats.

The subject of anchor-type is especially important to the big boat sailors. It is not something to dwell upon with a small boat. My first anchor was a coffee can filled with cement and had a ring bolt to tie my rope to (excuse me, my rode). I do not lose sleep worrying about the benefits of an Admiralty Kedge anchor versus a Danforth. A Navy Stockless and a Bruce is a comparison best left for the yacht club dining room. I have three anchors one of which is a Byers (I think), a mushroom, and a weird one that has a kind of roller on it. All three were salvaged from a small lake when the DNR drained it for bottom repairs to enhance fishing. One of them may have been mine originally. Type of anchor is not worth the firing of neurons. Another reason to love a small boat.

Scope of rode is insignificant since most of us small boaters are never in deep water. Writers expend gallons of ink wondering if you should use a 7:1 ratio or can they get by with 5:1. I loved college math, both times I had to take it. Ratios are not an element of my knowledge. As a small boat owner, I simply toss over the anchor over the side and wait until I don't move, then I give it a hard yank to see if it's set, and occasionally remember to tie off the rode. Small boat owners do not worry too much if they accidently forget to tie off the bitter end because we use cheap anchors from WalMart that cost about ten bucks.

The bigger the boat, the more expensive it is to keep it. Slips can run up from $15 per foot. Hoisting a large boat is expensive, time consuming, and a general pain. For us small craft aficionados, we simply drive our cheap trailer into the water, load the boat, exit, tie our lovely boat down, and drive off. Admittedly, we do have to raise and lower our mast but most of us have found some gimmick to use or trick to make it less than a heart attack level of physical exertion.

If our boat needs paint, we can DIY over a weekend without a lot of fuss and bother. West Marine or any other major supply house will send you a catalog with pages of paint schemes, information on fixing dings, and a selection of brushes and rollers that will boggle your mind, as if it wasn't boggled already. With a 42-footer you need an expensive outhaul, professional sanding, repair, and painting. There went this year's Social Security payments.

In the realm of large boats, snobbery is not only expected, it seems mandatory. The owners usually belong to a lavish yacht club with dining area where they can show off their sailing togs. They have spent a small fortune on rain gear, foul weather gear, tropical gear, and shore wear. They drink fine wines, and they probably have a boating version of a wine cellar.

Those of us who sail small boats do not have to spend a great deal of our life's saving on gear. We typically wear a ratty set of shorts, a tee-shirt from a concert we attended 17 years ago, and a pair of canvas sneakers straight from WalMart. Our old John Deere cap functions well. We have a cooler that says Pioneer Seed on it that holds our sodas and candy bars (we should know better than have adult beverages while sailing). When our day is done, we do not have to wear blazer and tie, we simply go to our favorite waterside bar where everyone is dressed in old clothes. The hamburgers are usually large, cheap, and delicious at such places. Beer is not craft brew but nationally recognized suds like PBR or Miller Lite. If you have to drink fancy, you get Budweiser.

Every small boat owner knows people like Mississippi Bob Brown, or Foxy Ryan, or someone of that ilk who has been around small lakes and rivers their whole life, built more boats than you have fingers and toes for calculations. They taught themselves and know more about boats than Columbus or Magellan.

Oh, you can have your Pacific Seacraft 37's and your Catalina 30's, but I want to be around Potters, Scamps, Montgomerys, and dinghies. I like being around guys who will quickly lend you a hand or a screwdriver. I like leaving my boat with a bunch of others and not having to worry about someone stealing something. They may borrow something, but they will bring it back. No PhD needed to have fun and enjoy the day. We just enjoy our lives without trying to outmatch the next guy. Yup, give me a small boat.

> Yes, I must go down to the lake today, to the lovely deep blue sky,
> And all I ask is gentle breeze to set my sails and fly.
> And the tiller kicks, Pandora sings, and my hands get to shaking.
> A dying fog's mist sets my white beard quaking.
>
> I must go down to the lake again for the call of the wildest loon
> Is a wild call and a clear call that may not be denied;
> And all I ask is a bit of wind and white clouds flying,
> And a cooler full of good draft beer, and the black birds crying.

I LOVE SMALL BOATS

I must go to the lake again, to the vagrant gypsy life,
To the bologna's way and the cracker's way where you need a whetted knife.
And all I ask is tall tale yarn from a laughing fellow sailor,
And a quick drink and a good laugh before you put your boat on the trailer.

~ apologies to John Masefield.

SIXTEEN

POLYSYLLABIC OBNUBILATE VERBIAGE

Sundry years ago, I had the questionable pleasure of working under an educational curriculum supervisor who proffered a multitude of polysyllabic phrases less intended to present exemplary wisdom than to obfuscate, confuse, and display his vocabulary de jour. We mere mortals under his jurisdiction would prepare for monthly meetings by mulling through a thesaurus, selecting obscure words, developing them into ludicrous statements, and even meshing the statements into questions for Doctor Dictionary to answer. Oh, how great the joy we had at taxpayers' expense while he chattered aimlessly to incomprehensible questions.

I suffer the same feelings reading various boating magazines and books. Since I barely comprehend the difference between a ketch and a yawl, I sputter to myself when some old salt peppers his/her article with nautical jargon. Patrick O'Brian immediately comes to mind. I had to purchase a book "Sea of Words" just to understand what the heck he was blabbering about. Not knowing the difference between a capybara and a carina left me unable to dribble a distich on a daedal.

Those of you who read my ancient article about "Ropes" know that I suffer from a prodigious paucity of sailing language. The first year or two of sailing I kept quiet around boat folks fearing that I would disclose my ignorance. My good friend Mississippi Bob Brown finally explained that asking questions is a good thing because if you don't know a stay from a shroud, you are probably going to end up in trouble. Worse, if you don't know a nautical reefer from a hippie reefer you could end up in jail.

Period of oscillation is not my wife's monthly mood swings nor are Knights the football team for Davenport Assumption high school. Or so Bob explained. Shafting is not the talent of inner office or intra office politics (an art form at which I was both experienced and brilliant). Punt evidently is not what you do on fourth down in football; although I did punt a life vest across the lake when my motor came off the transom and stuck upright in the mud. Actually, it was a damn fine punt worthy of the Green Bay Packers or the Detroit Lions.

My Navy days (during which they shipped me off to the Army for three years) I did learn that a Mustang is a former enlisted man now promoted to the officer ranks. Silly me spent some leave time at Mustang Ranch in Nevada thinking it was an enlisted men's club. Two days later I learned my mistake. Either that makes me one really slow learner or one very wise swabby.

Sweat Boards was an experience I thought I understood from my oral defense of my dissertation and written comprehensive examinations before the graduate boards. Unfortunately, the Sailor's Illustrated Dictionary notes differently. The book also notes that a "heeling magnate" is not the little wristbands that golfers wear to ward off shanks (a golf shank I know, an anchor shank is another story). A Great Coat I also understand; t'is a great description of the Pea Coat that is about as great as they get in Iowa's winters. But why the hell is a really warm coat called a PEA coat. Doesn't seem very vegetable- like to me.

Now I have a splendid hobby. I select a myriad of nautical, salty, and seafaring words and phrases, and I use them on the gang at the Tic Toc Tap, where we attempt to rid our minds of the cold and ice. They all believe I am indeed a true sailor of significant experience, a scholar of high esteem, and a wonderful conversationalist. Although it may be possible that they perceive me a total horses a--! I care little as long as someone else pays for the round.

Nevertheless, it would be nice if I did know the difference among a jolly boat, a launch, and a cutter. Reading O'Brian, Lambdin, and others of such ilk would be a lot more enjoyable if I knew a snow from brig, a sloop from a xebec, or even a Danforth from a plow. Believe me, I am a rural boy from Iowa, and snow and plow have little to do with water in my vocabulary.

My apple stern is dragging. Oh, to be a bear that I may hibernate until spring when I can rouse myself and set sail -- in spite of my lack of nautical lucidness. But for the fun of it, try utilizing some of the following in the next boating conversation.

- Brail up
- Woolding
- Calipee
- Peter-Boat
- To make boards
- Judas door
- Royal pole
- Pucker string
- Union gear

Now soak your captain's hat in salt water to dull and tarnish the gold piping. You are an Old Salt.

SEVENTEEN

KENNEBUNKPORT AND OTHER RARE DISEASES

Being a flooded cornfield sailor in Iowa, I remain bemused by the plethora of nautical equipment, phrases, events, and places that do not exist in my lexicon of English; nor, I am comfortable in assuring you, are they in the vocabulary of any self-respecting corn loving, pig-farming good old boy. *Messing About in Boats* was one of my loves and addictions; but too often I was confronted with words that escape me.

Tillers come from John Deere, are painted green, and keep the fields nice and neat. Oh, it might be argued that a Massy Ferguson or International tiller can be found on nondescript farms of the 120 acres variety. Why any fool would think of putting a good tiller in water is beyond me. The paint will come off and it will rust. Worse, it might not be fit for field duty.

The spare-the-rod-spoil-the-child Sisters of the Presentation of the Blessed Virgin Mary proclaimed that holding a gudgeon was a sin and probably a mortal one at that meaning that we better be darn careful in our lives until Confession, or the Sweat Box as we called it, on Saturday afternoon. In spite of a fully Catholic upbringing, I occasional hold a gudgeon against some idiots like those who talk on cell phones, drink coffee or pop, fiddle with the radio, read the paper, put on make-up, and smoke while attempting to drive. Frankly, I'd like to do more to those folks before they multiply than simply hold a gudgeon against them.

Bucksport, I understand. We have always gone out in our pick-ups, had a few beers, shined flashlights into the woods, and hammered the heck out of some hapless deer. Yup, Bucksport. I personally like a good old-fashioned 12-gauge shotgun but my best buddy subscribes to the notion that nothing will out kill a 50-cal. rifle with night light scope; although I can't help but wonder how the night scope works while we have the flashlights in the buck's eyes.

Little brother Mike is a scuba fanatic who cannot survive a couple of months without a little trip to salt water, warm air, and good rum. He can indeed tell the difference between the Windward and Leeward Islands, has great tales of adventures in Bonaire, got lost in a deep-water cavern in Cozumel (well, to be honest, it was me who got lost), and spent a gazillion dollars in the Caribbean. He thinks Jamaica is not worth a cold beer nor is Bimini. You can imagine my chagrin when wonderful editor Bob Hicks tells me that he is printing a piece about installing a Bimini top. I am sure that he meant Bikini top, and cannot comprehend why such an article is appropriate in MAIB; however, I volunteer for such a task.

Either Bob or I have totally failed geography class. He, poor old demented but lovable chap, insists that Augusta, Norway, Rochester, Madison, and Lincoln are in Maine. My pity goes out to him when he stated that Waterville is a quaint little village in the woods. Blarney! Waterville is a hick little town full of ruffians and drunks who hang out at Rainbow Gardens dance hall on Saturday nights. Believe me. I have been there, I have made passes at Waterville girls, and I have been beaten silly in Waterville. It is in Iowa.

My MAIB is replete with comments of Falmouth. Harkening back to my days under the stern gaze of the nuns I used to confess falmouth. My mouth was about as fal as they come but nowhere near the verbiage that flowed with such fluidity as from Charlie Bresnahan or Larry Murphy. I painfully remember being a falmouth with my dad once. He backhanded me so hard it knocked me all the way down the aisle of the City of Los Angeles passenger train. I NEVER used that phrase again, even when thinking of those cell phone coffee-drinking drivers

Back up. The strong- willed Sisters of the Presentation of the Blessed Virgin Mary always had a stern gaze. It was not until I sailed my first dinghy that I discovered that stern meant rear, and those nuns certainly had eyes in the back of their heads hidden by that veil.

Poor old Bob Hicks and his cronies hail from New England and that explains all those weirdo names. First of all, I never could spell Massachusetts and can hardly pronounce it. What in the world is a Massachuseetes, Massachewsits, Mass....forget it. Thank God for Iowa and civil, understandable, old-fashioned flag waving, common names. I live in Cedar Rapids. Now that is an easily understood concept. The city is on rapids of the Cedar River. None of this Narragansett, Skowhegan, Millinocket gobbledygook. Our rivers are simple: Upper Iowa, Yellow, Red, Iowa, Cedar, Skunk, and Raccoon. Our lakes are Spirit Lake, Clear Lake, Rock Creek Lake, and the totally uniquely named Round Lake. Okoboji is an exception but all it has to offer is a lot of beer, an amusement park, and a ton of shops selling Okoboji University tee shirts. While it proffers no such college, the town's mayor took a Hs.D. (high school diploma).

What, pray tell is a Penobscot, Pawcatuck, or Willimantic? A Norwich is a terrier. My neighbor owns one that bit me in the tush recently. Connecticut is another off the wall kind of state like Massachewsits. What's with the Lyme stuff anyway? Limes go in my gin and tonic, and I have no difficulties with that. Limes are green. Period. NOOOO.

Connneckteecut must spell it with a "Y". They present to us Lyme, Old Lyme, East Lyme, North Lyme without bothering us with a West or South Lyme. Being a wild-eyed Irish Iowan; I have no understanding about all this directional stuff when it comes to names. Can't the New Englanders come up with original names? Have they no intelligence capable of generating unique city titles. Evidently not because we have Attleboro and North Attleboro; New Haven and North, East and West Haven. They are all near Mystic. Trust me, they are all rather mysterious and mystic.

Mom had her hip socket replaced but Mr. Hicks talks about Woonsocket, which shows up in none of dad's pharmacy or Grandpa's medical dictionaries. Miss Finland, my wife, bought me a wonderful recliner for my birthday. I watch the crop reports on TV in a very comfortable position from MY chair. I do not know much about upholstery but I am sure that it is Naugatuck and not real leather.

As much as Connecticut is probably a quaint little state with good sailing, it hardly shows up in my National Geographic Road Atlas. It shares a page with northern New York but the goodly publishers felt sorry for the state and included a special block for a city map of Stamford, certainly it is Stanford misspelled but with Connecticut sailors, who knows. Anyway, StaMford has Holly Pond who I know was a stripper in San Diego in my Navy days. But what makes me feel sorry for Connecticut is that while they get a city enlargement the map of StaMford showing a yellow block with the city name, Holly Pond (who deserves mention), Highway 76 and Interstate 95 bisected by #107 and a star noting the First Presbyterian Church. That's all. Cedar Rapids, Iowa, has several Presbyterian churches, a boatload of Lutheran houses of worship, a bevy of Catholic Churches, and a Methodist church in every quadrant but we are sprouting new Bible and Evangelical churches like dandelions in my yard.

When my cruising time comes, I do believe that Connecticut is a nice place to start. Somehow it sounds fun to sail from Saccham Head

(I have been called a dumb head but am clueless about a saccham), past the Thimbles and Short Beach (Iowa's beaches are in pretty short supply too), and land at Green Farms where I am confident I will feel comfortable and at home.

For some reason launching from Wequeteadock, drifting past Noank, and landing at Giant's Neck does nothing for me; although a quickie at Pleasure Beach might make it worth my while. At least I am not trying to tell my poor old Mother that I am sailing down the Quinnipiac River. I couldn't pronounce it. And you thought Mississippi was hard to spell.

Clearly the Connecticut people are different from the New Yorkers who can be seen as soon as you cross the border. New York folks named their towns after normal King's English nouns: Lake Carmel, Yorktown, Jefferson Valley, Pleasantville, Tarrytown, White Plains, Yonkers, and Harrison. No Lake Pocotopaug or Pachaug for New Yorkers. They are Americans.

All of this confoundment and confusion has made me hungry. Miss Unnaslahti of Saloranta herself left specific orders to make some stew for this evening's dining pleasure. I think of stew as pretty bland so I might add some pintles hoping she won't hold a gudgeon against me or deport me to Insomnia, Connecticut. Worse, if I don't eat properly, I might get Kennebunkport even though I am certain I was inoculated against that in the Navy. It happened right after a night with Holly Pond when I was out with Rocky Hill and the crew from South Glastonbury.

EIGHTEEN

JET SKIS AS WATER FOWL

In a Letter-to-the-editor that appeared in a small watercraft magazine, the writer questioned why the editor had long ignored jet skis. Clearly, he reasoned, jet skis were watercraft, and they were small: furthermore, they often utilized the same waterways. He additionally subscribed to the notion that since small boats and jet skis were of similar ilk, they should share the same journal. The editor diplomatically responded with a "NO!" He would remain a publisher about boats.

My initial reaction was in agreement with the editor especially since he has a backlog of decent boat articles over which he must judge and prioritize. But the Letter to the Editor author did spur my antiquated brain. Sundry thoughts and remembrances aroused slowly but profoundly. Jet Skis have proliferated along the Mississippi to an extent paralleling the nuisance Zebra mussels and Asian carp. Worse, they have infiltrated the nearby Cedar River that flows through my beloved town. The Cedar has less than two miles of navigable water and is appallingly narrow. Nevertheless, in an urban population of nearly 250,000 this river attracts hordes of Jon boats, houseboats, bass boats, runabouts, sailboats, and, of course, jet skis.

Gunwale to gunwale these entities roar around the lake with motors ranging from the fancy bass boats with twin 250s to small fishing jon boats with ancient 2.5 Evinrudes pushing them along. Add to this mix a myriad of skiers in age range from 4 to 80 following on boards at speeds from barely afloat to faster than I-80's speed limit. To say only that it is crowded is like saying there are only a few pigs in Iowa.

Not that I mind traffic on the river, boating around the Mississippi teaches one that crowds are inevitable and the standing law of the water is that the bigger the greater the right-of-way. Try sailing down on a 24-barge towboat and expecting the skipper to yield to your unpowered vessel!

I do remember one particular evening that I first purchased my beloved **Genny Sea**, a West Wight Potter 15, and had to move it from one trailer to another. Neighbor Mike and I towed the two trailers, launched the boat, and attempted to put the boat on the second trailer. About the time I managed to hook the boat to the winch line a pair of jetskiiers made a run at us at Mach 3, missing us by inches but creating waves of such magnitude that my little Potter jumped over the trailer guide rails and, because of its attachment to the winch, ended up on its beam ends. The skier's laughter faded into the ethers as my swearing rose to a level unheard in quantity or quality outside of boot camp (my company commander was a Senior Chief Boiler Tender who hadn't been ashore in decades, he could swear for 20 minutes without repeating himself).

This single event had enlarged my animosity toward those who ride those things. I have developed a prodigious hatred of all thing jet ski-ish, until I read that Letter-to-the-Editor. With significant thought about the problems of the city and state, I have prescribed the following concept:

Cogitating the dilemma, we Cedar Rapidians are facing since the Flood of 2008 in which over 5000 homes were damaged or destroyed, the entirety of downtown was under a story and a half of water, and all businesses and homes ten blocks on either side of the river for the length of the city were ruined, I have been looking for a fiscal opportunity to save our ravaged town. Worse, the state of Iowa that has a balanced budget mandate in the state constitution, is so broke that the Governor was forced to demand a 10% reduction across the board budget cut, and he will need to make another such demand before the fall's election (see if Governor Culver gets re-elected, not a chance). **(Note: he wasn't)**

The answer to many of these problems is in front of our eyes. We need a hunting season for jet skis! Think about it. First, the state can charge a small fortune for hunting licenses. Certainly, most of us would gladly pay upwards to $200 for the opportunity to take aim at such an elusive target. We pay half that to hunt deer, and most of them are as tame as milk cows. Not much sport there. But Jet Skiers are speedy little devils requiring great stealth, selection of good hunting spots, and a high-quality high-powered rifle with excellent scopes. Sport stores will reap barrels of money, sales taxes will rise appropriately, and the new sport will keep kids off the streets and joined in quality father-son time.

Think of the opportunities. Hunters will be rewarded with a bounty of say $10 for the ears of jet skiers. Gophers get you $.50, coyotes bring only a few bucks, and wolves aren't much better. With the bounty, hunters have a chance to recoup some money back on their expenses while the state is shed of waterway congestion while making money doing it. Furthermore, hunters should be allowed to salvage the jet skis. This will also boost the state economy due to the need for big, big retrievers and needed training. I think Newfoundland dogs or large black labs may serve this need. They have the strength and genetic orientation to swim out, grab the Jet Ski, and tow it ashore. Here the hunter can salvage aluminum, steel, plastic for re-cycling, and perhaps even some precious oil and gas. This means more money for the hunter and additional need for metal salvage companies.

Hunting jet skiers clearly would impact Iowa education. We have traditionally been among the top three states in various assessments including the SAT and ACT as well as the ubiquitous Iowa Test of Educational Development and the Iowa Test of Basic Skills, the two most solid and robust exams in the country. The elimination of dolts who ride jet skis will eventually raise the cumulative IQs of Iowa and rid us of this pestilence, but it also opens up the job market as their loss means more job openings.

Truly, I see great opportunities here with nothing but fiscal, social, and educational gains in the offing. I am so excited that I have proffered this concept to Governor Culver (who is in desperate shape since he must face a previous governor in the election, The Governor for Life Terry Branstad, a six-term predecessor). I also have examined the prospect of purchasing a quality 30.06 with laser vision and military scope.

*(This was previously published in **Messing About in Boats**, the editor added "Consider that perchance the jet skiers might choose to fight back with fly-by grenade tossing attacks on moored and slow-moving boats intruding on their turf!)*

NINETEEN

USS MARGARET

Hollywood gave us pink submarines, talking mules on boats, and skippers with chained down palm trees; but no screen writer, no Pulitzer Prize author, no Tony winning playwright could have dreamed up a comedy like the yacht, **MARGARET**, and the Suicide Fleet. This mess up could only have been the creation of middle ranking desk commanders, career Navy Department bureaucrats, and mindless Congressmen.

World War I broke out with technological horrors unimagined at the time. Submarine warfare caught America by surprise especially the Navy Department that had rusticated since the Civil War. The creative commanders of credenzas in the hallowed halls of the Navy Department rushed into paroxysms of novel ideas to combat those hated German submarines that could ungentlemanly sink ships without warning. While the destroyer became the vessel of choice, the U.S. had too few of them to counter the underwater terrorists. Some brilliant nautical genius decided the Navy needed sub-chasers. Since the budget or the building prohibited such a boat, these gurus of war decided to purchase old civilian yachts and convert them to be the cutting edge in anti-submarine warfare.

With a combination of great patriotic fervor tempered with greed, wealthy men of the East willingly sold their aged, decrepit yachts to the

Navy. A corporate CEO willingly offered the **MARGARET**, a 176-foot 250-ton boat with a tender beam of 21 feet, to the Navy. Well past her prime and too narrow for the open sea, **MARGARET** was appraised by the government at the munificent sum of $94,000 but the Navy paid the owner $104,000 for the top-heavy yacht noted for its wonderful wine compartment and dining room.

The quintessential wonders of naval architecture immediately chopped off the boats mast and bowsprit. To the already rolling **MAGGIE**, as she was quickly dubbed, they added a charthouse, pilot house, and winged bridge towering over the main deck. They also added 3" guns fore and aft and equipment for depth charges. With the amended weight distribution, the boat not only rolled badly but her stern sank significantly to the point that waves tended to wash over very leaky portholes. Needless to say, since the stern was constantly admitting water, that section became the enlisted men's quarters.

A recent Medal of Honor recipient, Frank Jack Fletcher, had wrangled himself onto the staff of uncle Admiral Frank Friday Fletcher's staff at Vera Cruz. Now that the war had commenced, he found himself on a dock in Mexico when his career possibilities were on ships in the Atlantic. Fletcher had heard about these yacht-to-subchaser ships and pulled every string he could to obtain a command. His friends had suddenly turned from their backwater jobs to great assignments. Their envy of his Medal of Honor became his envy as buddies Chester Nimitz, Ray Spruance, and Bill Halsey headed off to war. Fletcher finally received his wish: command of the **MARGARET**.

His joy turned to disillusionment when he found **MARGARET**. Her officers were all new to the Navy and had no sailing experience. A recent clothing salesman was quickly appointed gunnery officer, medical officer, and supply officer. Fletcher immediately ordered a trial for his ship and her crew. He instantly grew to regret this decision as **MAGGIE** quickly lost power against the current, smashed the pier, fouled the anchor and tore out the anchor stanchion. The elderly boat could not generate enough power to counter a harbor current. At best, she could eke out a meager 6 knots but 4 knots was her usual speed. Fletcher discovered that she was frightfully tender requiring an additional 35 tons of ballast according to his own calculations. Unfortunately, his ship had no space for 35 tons of ballast but Fletcher found nooks and crannies for 5 tons. Worse, he realized he could not steam out of the way of his own depth charges; therefore, he ordered that depth charges would not be fired.

At the subsequent commissioning ceremony Fletcher's spic-and-span crew watched as **MARGARET'S** flag proudly was raised, albeit upside down -- the universal signal for needing assistance. Fletcher joined sister yachts in as bad of condition as his own that the enlisted men immediately dubbed The Suicide Fleet.

Being prepared to fight the foe, Fletcher ordered gunnery drills. A second regret. The fore gun fired and subsequently blew out the forecastle locker door. The aft gun was fired and it blew out the stern rail, flooded the enlisted men's quarters and sprung 19 leaks in the hull. Both guns were sprung from the deck.

The ship was so tender that 59 of 61 crew members seasick. Fletcher ordered that his men not be allowed to sleep on deck for fear of losing them overboard so he sent them to their wet, leaky, cold quarters. When **MAGGIE'S** condenser died and her steerage gear sheared, Fletcher was forced to send his puking men to manually steer the boat through a series of ropes and pulleys. If that weren't enough, **MAGGIE** ran out of coal half way to the Bahamas. With no power, pumps, communications, or lights Fletcher was forced to request a tow. In the process of setting up a towline while a bucket brigade hauled water from the interior, his starboard anchor abruptly dislodged and 105 fathoms of chain disappeared into the Atlantic.

Fletcher finally arrived in the Bahamas but his request for materials and supplies were blatantly rejected. No supply officer would hazard important equipment on the Suicide Fleet. His own supply officer was sent ashore with some trusted crewmen known for keeping secrets. Their orders were simply to find the necessary supplies on the list. Period. No questions asked. They did nicely.

The fleet of whacky boats was ordered to the Azores, if they could make it. Fletcher's request for food was also rejected. **MAGGIE** and her sisters were, to be blunt, expendable. Nevertheless, Fletcher's sheep wandered off to the Atlantic. At one point he received communications of a submarine sighting. Rushing off at a roaring 4 knots the fleet never found the submarine. With bald impunity the German submarine radioed in the clear and in English that he had spotted the **MAGGIE** but thought her unworthy of a torpedo or shells.

Fletcher and the Suicide fleet reached the Azores in spite of untold issues. The Azores Department commander, A.W. Osteshans, reviewed the **MARGARET** and reported the deck leaked, crew quarters were uninhabitable, the condenser was beyond repair, her steam drums could not attain but half the needed pressure, and her 5/16th inch drums were worn down to under 1/16 inch. His report stated, "… this ship was not meant for sailing out of sight of land or, I might say, out of Long Island Sound… To sum up in a few words, I consider the **MARGARET** nothing but a piece of junk, and I cannot imagine a ship being bought for the government that is so worthless for the duty required."

MARGARET survived as a storage facility in the Azores. She was junked for $1,200. Frank Jack Fletcher received orders to relieve his friend, William Halsey, as commanding officer of the **USS BENHAM**, a destroyer in top shape. In World War II Fletcher commanded the Task Forces at Coral Sea and Midway. He was the senior Naval officer for the landings at Guadalcanal. Northern Japanese islands surrendered to him on his flagship **PANAMINT** as the government surrendered on the **USS MISSOURI** in Tokyo harbor.

But **MAGGIE** lived on in the memories of her officers and crew. Her adventures enlivened many parties at Fletcher's home or sundry Officers Clubs. One former Ensign even wrote a book about **MAGGIE** and the Suicide Fleet. Hollywood missed a great comedy.

For further reading:

Prosper Buranelli, Maggie of the Suicide Fleet (1930).
Stephen D. Regan, In Bitter Tempest, the biography of Admiral Frank Jack Fletcher (1994).
Stephen D. Regan, "When Frank Jack Fletcher Met Maggie" Naval History, (February 2011)
The Papers of Frank Jack Fletcher, University of Wyoming.

TWENTY

ANXIOUS, DEPRESSED, OBSESSIVE-COMPULSIVE SAILOR IN THE WINTER

Anxious, depressed, obsessive-compulsive? Yes, I am, and I have the psychiatric reports, prescription bills, and bitten nails that attest to it, to say nothing of a frazzled wife, a screwed-up pet pug who thinks he is human, and a cat that wants to join a squirrel colony. But I am also Irish and have me saintly father's wit and blarney to entertain the lost souls who buy me beer at the TIC TOC when the temperature plummets below zero. Unfortunately, beer and blarney can only last so long. So, I try to keep my winter sailing misery to a minimum by doing things shiply (if that indeed be a word, if not, it should be).

An immodest wind blew down a hardy maple limb from my neighbor's tree, and he, in a kindly mood, sawed it up in smaller pieces for my fireplace. I eyed one foot long absolutely solid hunk of maple and determined it had better use than ash and soot. With Bolger, Poole, and a myriad of other ship builders in mind, I decided that this wood needed desperately to be fashioned into a model sailboat.

THE WORLD'S WORST SAILOR

By gently peeling the bark and then stripping the wood lengthwise I had the early perspective of a little hull. Michelangelo once said that his Moses already existed in perfection while still a pillar of marble; all he had to do was knock off the excess stone. My little boat was the same, or so I thought.

First, I had to rough out the hull. This required the purchase of a Dremel set and a plethora of bits, router bits, sanding blocks, and polishing wheels. I also bought the router kit. Since I had never worked with wood before (hey, they would not let me take woodworking or such things in high school because some counselor decided I was destined to be a pharmacist which provides good evidence of why I ended up with degrees in history, English, Counseling, Psychology, and Education but can't tell an aspirin from a stool softener and can't hammer a nail). Anyway, never being totally rash, I immediately started to hew out the interior of the hull. Lesson One was that you have to have the damn wood well anchored in order to do the routing or your end up with a multitude of dents, errors, scratches, etc. I figured this is why God invented paint: to cover up our screw ups.

Once the hull was completed to perfection (or close enough for government work); I ran to the local craft store to figure out a paint scheme. Examining the array of sizes and colors I was bumped by a little girl in a total screaming fit that only a 3-year-old can exhibit and an exasperated and bewildered mother who had no clue how to deal with the child (is there really anyway to deal with a child's fit?). Being old, gray bearded, grandfatherly in nature I got on my knees and looked the girl right in the eye and asked her if she could help me. This stranger at her eye level immediately drew her attention away from whatever was causing her tantrum. I asked her if she could pick a color for me because I had built a small little boat and didn't know what I should paint it. She instantly ran behind her mother, but from around mom's knees peeked a big brown eye. I again asked the question. No response. I asked her what her favorite color was. After a lengthy silence she muttered, "Yellow". So, I asked her to point to a yellow color she liked, and she grabbed a spray can with a yellow lid.

Mother, by this time, was thanking me profusely and God Blessing me. The first I appreciated and the latter I probably needed. I picked up the can of paint and then, still on my aching knees, asked the girl for a good name for my boat. She of course was still anchored behind mom but with a little coaxing she told me her name was Grace. I promised the girl I would name my model after her. So now you know how my little Sea Grace came to be named. For the record, several customers and clerks thanked me for my ability to stifle a temper tantrum. Now, if I could carve or sail that well.

I made the mast tiller, and bowsprit from a little leftover dowel lying on the floor of the garage. I took some of the pieces of maple scrapped from the hull and fashioned the center board and the rudder. Finally, the stand was made from some pieces of oak sawn from the too tall appliance garage I bought for Mama for Christmas.

Being a total idiot and terminally confused and needing a sail, I took an old pillow case labeled PENNSYLVANIA HOSPITAL, a cloth evidently lifted from the dorm in Philadelphia by my beloved first mate and wife who got her medical technology degree there about 45 years ago. I figured it was time for it to be put to good use besides covering the dog's pillow. I figured if junior high girls could use a sewing machine, I certainly should have no difficulties with the Singer.

Wrong. First of all, you have to trim the cloth in a triangle. Sister Mary Annette never allowed me a pair of scissors in the first or second grades, and Sister Marie Therese kept all sharp objects from my reach in 6th and 7th grades. Now I understand why. Not only can I not figure out a triangle, I can't cut worth a damn. Not a problem, says I; I can hem it to even it up.

The Singer was set up, the fabric kind of folded into a triangular shape, and away I whirred. I always wondered why Miss Frozen Finland herself had so many pins. Evidently you need to pin the fabric rather than just sort of fold it over. And what the heck is that bobber thingy and why can't Singer make a machine that sews in a straight line? After using up the entire pillow case and all scrape fabric in the house including a handkerchief or two, I went to the fabric store and bought about 3 yards of white cloth. Experimentation finally yielded some shaped semblance to a sail.

Thus, now brightly colored and over the mantel amongst the vast array of nautical decorations resides the **Sea Grace** in awesome splendor. Ok, the thing is not going to be in the Naval Museum in Washington nor even on the shelf of a anyone special; however, building this little piece did keep me sane for several weeks. And, after several glasses of beer, it looks almost good.

TWENTY-ONE

FLORIDA RUMINATION

You can distinguish native Floridians from snowbirds when the temperature is around 70 degrees; the Floridians are bundled up like Eskimos in midwinter and the snowbirds are wearing shorts and Hawaiian shirts. Today was one of those days and we went beach walking with other folks from Minnesota, Ohio, and Canada.

Snowbirds must collect shells as if they are unique to the world and precious entities not unlike diamonds and pure gold. These will be brought home in plastic sacks, washed and cleansed and sanitized fit for surgery and placed on the driveway where eventually they will be shoveled with the snow out onto the streets and plowed to God knows where.

I do not know a lightening whelk from Lawrence Welk or a quahog from a mussel. One Iowa state senator complained that the endangered Higgins Eye clam couldn't possibly be endangered because anytime someone wanted to build a marina or dock or shore-side building they will inevitably stumble on Higgins Eye clams. Iowans on the Mississippi side and the Missouri River side have fought those damn clams for years. I wouldn't recognize one from a Sailor's Ear. I probably have pried open several of these rare creatures for bait.

With water, water everywhere, I scan the island for marinas and docks to saunter around like I belong there in order to examine sailboats of sundry varieties. Today Ms. Frozen Finland set the Order of the Day to include grocery store shopping. Arriving at Publix (the ubiquitous grocery chain in Florida) I noticed a several sailboats behind the store. Ms. Saloranta was left to herself among the fresh vegetables while I sneaked out to view the boats.

Three Morgan ketches of various sizes up to 72 feet sat awaiting customers who pay goodly sums with the faint hope of heading into the Gulf and actually seeing a porpoise (or dolphin—don't ask me the difference). I have no clue how to sail a ketch but I did seriously threaten to steal one and attempt to run it up the Mississippi river to Iowa. The lady at the dock had a good laugh and said she would gladly take me out on the Gulf--if I paid for 4 people at $40 per head. If it weren't raining, I'd have taken her up on the offer. I did manage to get back in the grocery store to assist Ms. I-Hate-Sailing with the bags.

The Gulf shall be invaded by this Dinghy Captain if only to annoy Mississippi Bob who is skillfully crafting yet another work of art that belongs in a museum instead of on the water. Bob's boats, canoes, and kayaks are beautiful; but I'd never tell him that. Worse, they are delightful on the water smoothly knifing through the lakes, cleaving waves, and more balanced than the workings of a Swiss watch. Of course, I am beyond envious of his talent and knowledge but being a stubborn Iowa Irishman, I'll never, ever admit this in public. I feel a moral necessity to harass Bob by sending him an e-mail talking about warm weather, nice water, and sunshine knowing full well that Apple Valley, MN is barely making 0 degrees while buried under several inches of snow which will continue for at least another 10 days. Eat your heart out, Bob!

I finally convinced Ms. Frozen Tundra to take a small afternoon dolphin-watching cruise on a Morgan 52 that nearly blinded me with the glare off highly polished teak and sparking stainless steel everywhere but the internal beauty of the cabin was ignored for a more sunny and ideal watch post on the bow where I made an ass of myself naming all the rigging and gadgets within sight. I could not help it. Shiny Lewmar wrenches and Harken furlers need to be examined and noticed to say nothing of the sundry lifeline ornamentation and safety equipment, and to mention that while the ketch had sails unfurled and the jib flying, the captain also had his engine running for faster reaction time in case of a whale sighting or a Canadian overboard. The sole crew member who was to provide free colas and fruit drinks should anyone desire one (and frankly at the prices charged, a free drink could have been champagne) but said Tar was rarely seen and sat displaying an "attitude" only moving to tie up at the end of the trip and hold up a large bucket for tips. I want her job.

To keep myself from significant withdrawal symptoms, I rationed my winter boating magazines for reading while on vacation. I failed at keeping *Messing About In Boats* that had to be read immediately upon arrival partially because it contained an article that I had written. *Wooden Boat, Small Craft Advisor, Cruising Outpost* and *Good Old Boat* were the rationed editions. I mulled through the first magazine during week one by re-reading each article twice and admiring the photography earnestly but it barely kept me from craziness until the week passed and I could delve into *Good Old Boat*, a Twin Cities periodical of wonderful DIY information and proffers some attention to the Great Lakes unlike *SAIL* or others or that ilk; furthermore, editor Karen Larson has been very nice to me but declining to print anything written by me. Unfortunately, my appetite was greater than my wise planning and the journal was swallowed in toto while my wife went for a walk. I will have to go through this again scouring the ads for interesting concepts.

For "book" reading I have selected several for the month including Steinbeck's incredible *Cannery Row*, Larsson's *Girl who Played with Fire*, a Jack Higgins spy thriller, Cowling's the *Captain's Story*, plus a Sea-story Mega pack of short stories that have some connection with the water, and Mark Twain's incredible *Life on the Mississippi*, an all-American classic.

Having never read that particular Twain story, it was high on my to-do list but it had slipped my mind for several years until I stumbled on an article that insisted this was worthy of consuming; plus, it was free (or very cheap) on KINDLE that is so easy when traveling. I grew up on the Mississippi river and had drowned worms in her sloughs, left a rather jaunty cap in the channel, and watched barges by the thousands before heading to college. I canoed under a bridge over a backwater area and saw a hand painted sign reading "Dan Regan, USN 1939". My dad was only a junior in high school at that time and would indeed join the Navy in early 1941 before requesting assignment with the Fleet Marines in the fall of that year before Pearl Harbor because he wanted to see something of world and San Diego was getting pretty boring. His wishes came true and his 9th Marines got the pleasure of visiting with the Japanese on Bougainville and Guam but was sent home as an element of a new Marine division that never was formed and missed Iwo Jima where his former unit suffered overwhelming casualties.

Nevertheless, life along the Mighty Mrs. Sippy is as unique as a seafarer's café in New England providing river folk personalities, tall tales, tons of history, a specific definition as to manhood, and a love of the water that land people cannot possibly comprehend – a style that has not changed for 150 years, albeit a bit more technological. The stories in a typical river bar could fertilize Iowa for a generation. Frustrated drop-out university professors sit beside junior high dropout fishermen complaining about whatever is the topic of the day, dentists chat with toothless locals about fish they only dreamed of catching, and someone always has a get-rich-quick scheme which, on occasion, is actually a get-rich-scheme such as buying a bunch of lots on a sand pile in the 1950s that is now Padre Island.

Samuel Clemens (ok, Mark Twain) wrote with sagacity with humor, a sense of devotion, and a style hammered out through experience in river town newspapers and a great imagination. Although Tom Sawyer and Huckleberry Finn may have earned the great prizes of literature, *Life On the Mississippi* is observably one of the best-written books in our language, displaying an artistry of sentence development, paragraph structure, and thematic evolution while tossing in sidebars of pure American experience and humor. This is the book that is a must for students of Writing and Literature.

If you haven't read it, do so. Try it out in the winter while awaiting sailing weather or set anchor, pop a beer, and enjoy it on the water. My Florida trip was significantly better because of Twain's book.

TWENTY-TWO

SAILING THINGS THAT REALLY P@#%&* ME OFF

Our bathroom was the long-time repository of one of those silly one-liner joke books called 1001 Things That P@#%* Me Off. Being of a simple mind and easily amused, I found the book not only humorous but also startlingly similar to my annoyances. My Finnish wife thought the book silly, stupid, and (God forbid) a collector of dust; ergo, Ms. Dour Universe 1973, tossed it. In her honor, I posit the following sailing things that P@#%&* Me Off:

1. JET SKIS. If God had really wanted us to scoot around the lake at 70 mph, He would have put more oomph in Five Bean Chili. Downing 6 Buds in 20 minutes, straddling a machine that serves no purpose in this universe, and then attempting to swamp sail boats, scare hell out of fishermen (OK, fisher-PEOPLE you politically correct snobs -- which is another thing that really P@#%&*s me off), worry swimmers, and kill off a quiet afternoon on the water is a person who should have been flushed down the toilet at birth. Mea Culpa Monsignor Friedl; I'll say an Act of Contrition but I won't mean it. Jet Ski people make perfect target practice for owners of 30-06 rifles. There should be a bounty for Jet Ski people.

2. BIG BASS BOATS. My little 12-foot dinghy, **ZONONA**, likes the water of Pleasant Creek Lake (kind of a contradiction, isn't it? Is it a lake or is it a creek? Hey, it's Iowa). In my canoe or my brother's kayak, I can circle the lake in about 90 minutes. I just love those simpletons who bring out their $75,000 SUV hauling a $35,000 metallic red bass boat with a 200 hp Merc replete with radar, sonar, depth finder, under water TV camera, digital wind gauge, short-wave radio, lap-top computer with the latest weather reports and navigation charts, hydraulic anchors fore and aft, and a half ton of carbon fiber poles, Rapala lures, and titanium hooks just to catch a handful of blue gill or crappies, hardly enough to serve as hor d'overes for "Ms. Lapland ". I love it when the little kid fishing off a point using a cane pole and freshly dug worms catches the Tiger Muskie while Captain Dimwit in his $100,000 worth of fishing machine comes home with a snarl and a snag. By the way, what the hell do you need a 200 hp motor for anyway???

3. NAUTICA MODELS. I just hate the cruiser types with expensive boat shoes, tailored trousers, and monogrammed shirts. They wear $45 per ounce cologne and have towels in the head that are color coordinated with the interior of their boat that was selected by a "color counselor". All their lines are color coordinated too. They have a dry cleaner on speed dial at every port, have never managed a stain on their contemptible shirts, and just love handing out 3 color business cards with their boat's name on it. Hell, even their swimsuits and robes are monogrammed with their boat's name. They invariably have personal names like Buffy or Biff, and they are soooo WASP that it makes my Irish blue-collar Catholic blood boil. They are usually lawyers.

4. LACK OF DIRECTIONS. Why is it that every single piece of sailing equipment comes without any directions? Am I the only beginner in the world? My beautiful dinghy came in a nice crate with no directions on rigging or even a reminder to plug the pit cock. I looked at pictures and figured it out for myself. My boat trailer came in pieces with no

directions and I am still fiddling with it 2 years later. The depth finder had no directions nor did the GPS; both are toys every dinghy sailor floating around in a puddle absolutely need. Right? I have, therefore, been forced to double my expenses by purchasing a plethora of books on rigging, sailing, knots, repairing (as if we rookies don't mess up), and even a damn nautical dictionary because I don't know a roodle from a rose box nor a pintle from a gudgeon.

5. YUPPIE SAILING BEER FANATICS. These less than welcome guests can literally sit and yap about beer for hours and hours on end. They actually know the difference and care about the differences between lager and pilsner beers to say nothing of ales, stouts, bocks, and any other kind of liquid posing as a beer. They delight in a trivia game whereby you name a country and they can name the top national beer of that nation. These bores would never cross the stoop of any dining establishment that didn't sell Koff dark, Harp on tap, or Dos Eques dark AND light. These foul Yuppies honestly understand the distinction between Point beer and Leinenkugel and can sound like an idiot wine freak in their descriptions of beer. "Point has the pungent taste of pine mediated by a smoky oak nose tinged with a modicum of grain." Their conversations are dull and boring and consistent and predicable. To the question, "What beer do I personally choose?" the sole answer is of course, "The cheapest." What ever happened to Blatz, Grain Belt, Falstaff, and Hamms? And as far as I am concerned, Point beer tastes like panther pee and rust water. I'll drink Koff in Finland where it is cheap. I do drink Bud because I own ANHEUSER-BUSCH stock.

6. NON-SAILING RELATIVES. Wives who see no redeeming value in boats, water, or sails; mothers who believe that all money spent on boats is wasteful; brothers who think that REAL men have REAL boats (i.e., big motors); and children who complain that their inheritance is being sunk into plywood and fiberglass should all be tied to heavy anchors and shoved over the side. The good news is that the boat takes me away from all their carping and whining. When my wife,

bellyaching about my not raking the leaves, made the mistake of going into the bathroom, I stealthily hooked up the boat and headed to the lake. The wind freshened and the leaves flew over to the neighbor's lawn. I avoided work AND got a day on the lake. She found no humor in the situation.

7. WINTER. The next person who says, "Oh, I just love the snow." shall be punched in the nose. There is no value meteorologically, ecologically, psychologically, morally, or spiritually in winter. God just invented winter to P@#%&* us off. My neighbor gets a silly grin all over his puss as he brazenly revs up his snowmobile, rushes off in a blast of noise and flying ice, and returns with frostbitten extremities and a missing child probably lost in one of the myriad of snow drifts he feels an abnormal necessity to plow though. I have a doctorate in psychology. He is nuts. Believe me. Meanwhile my little dinghy sits covered with snow, her lovely lines obliterated in the ice, her sails stuffed in a bag in the basement, and her rudder hanging sadly in the garage while I gulp huge quantities of Paxil, Xanax, Trazadone, and alcoholic beverages to tolerate the time until I can hit the water -- which I do as soon as any water stands open in the ice.

8. MINNESOTA AND WISCONSIN. See #7. Why is it that the two states with the most lakes have 10 months of snow and ice? Why is it that the two states with the best sailing in the world also have the world's largest and most numerous mosquitoes? Why is it that the two states that proliferate the world's most curvaceous and beautiful blonde women force them to be covered up with parkas and boots? Worse, both states love hockey. There is no rational thinking that defends hockey except that it makes all the dentists happy. Sailors usually have all their teeth, feel no intense desire to whack people over the head with a stick, or to chase little hard rubber things on ice. Sailors sit back and enjoy life. Peacefully and quietly. Why is it that so many people who live in Minnesota and Wisconsin don't deserve Minnesota or Wisconsin?

9. TOO MANY BOAT MAGAZINES. Did you ever try to balance your checkbook and wonder where the heck all the money went (excluding boat expenses which are really under the category of "gifts of love")? Check the floor beside your recliner or your bed. I'll bet dollars to donuts you'll find *Messing About in Boats, Shallow Water Sailor, Good Old Boat, Wooden Boat, Latitudes and Attitudes, Sail,* and *Small Craft Advisor.* Oh sure, a hundred others exist but they aren't on my floor. Darn it! I love these things and have to read and re-read them all several times and wish I could afford many more. They have so much information totally superfluous to my needs, so expensive, so unnecessary, but so much fun. I am addicted, that is why I have to see a shrink. I have to tolerate my wife's yelling at me after another magazine appears in the mailbox. I have to deal with getting nothing accomplished. But I cannot live without Bob Bitchin's humor, Karen Larson's scribbling about her Mega 30, Bob Hick's attention to detail, etc. etc. The fact that they do not come often enough P@#%&* me off!

10. WIND. Wind is the absolute necessity for sailing (well, duh!). I find it outrageously frustrating to discover that good winds blow on the days I have to work and can't be found for love nor money when I have the day off. Wind is my particular nemesis. Too often on a lovely day when the sun is shining, the breeze is fresh, my wife suddenly decides to spend the day on the water, and all is well in the universe, the wind suddenly either slackens to a mere whisper; or else it decides to rev up to a near gale force whereby dinghies keel over, only butt heads venture on the lakes, birds suddenly disappear, and even the DNR won't come near the water. I have tried everything. I pray to Neptune. I wear a St. Elmo medal. I put a St. Christopher medal under the mast step. I sprinkle holy water all over my boat. Nope, Mother Nature alone decides when and how much wind she shall proffer, and rarely does she take me into account. In fact, I am beginning to believe that Mother Nature doesn't like me at all. That has to be my top all-time thing that REALLY P@#%&* me off.

TWENTY-THREE

NAUTICAL TERMS

The terminology and slang of sailors is confusing, fun, weird, and occasionally humorous. While reading the 20 books of Patrick O'Brian series, I was so confounded by the naval terms and jargon that I had to purchase a special book, **Sea of Words**, edited by Dean King, a mere 483-page lexicon in order to comprehend the books. Unfortunately, it was only a sample of the nautical vernacular. Over the years I have collected several nautical dictionaries.

ARGOSY: A large merchant vessel usually found in Poland or Venice, or a men's magazine.

CACHEXY: Malnutrition or wasting disease or a hot-looking Czech gal.

JIB OF JIBS: The 6th jib on a bowsprit or a new jib after the old one blows out.

FLY: The length from staff to the extreme edge of a flying flag or the Minnesota state bird.

PUDDING: Oakum and cordage that wreaths the bow of a ship to avoid chafing, quite similar to the dessert served at Catholic elementary schools.

ABLE WHACKETS: A game played where the loser is given a whack with a knotted handkerchief, also given by nuns to children whose homework was eaten by the dog.

DEAD MEN: Also known as Irish pennants, a term for loose strings or pieces of cordage, also known when your mom finds out you were out parked with Suzie instead of studying at the library.

LANDSHARK: A derisive term for lawyer about whom there is only one joke, the rest are all true.

LEATHERNECK: A piece of leather surrounding a Marine's neck to protect him from sword thrusts or the neck of a sailor who has been at sea too long.

NIP CHEESE: An expression describing the purser's propensity to keep some of the supplies for his own use to sell, or the kind of cheese used in school hot lunch programs with stale macaroni.

NANTUCKET JOY RIDE: An enlightening term that accurately describes the ride in a whaleboat after spearing a whale, or spoiled New England rich kids racing their Corvettes.

JACKKNIFE: A hinge bladed knife used by officers while crew used a sheath knife, or it is what my brother did with his truck. In the 50's, every boy carried a jackknife. Today a child will automatically be expelled for carrying a jackknife.

LASSIE: A body found on the beach and believed dead until a sailor's dog kept whining over the body that was found to be still alive. The sailor was John Lassie, and so is every longhaired Collie in the universe.

NAUTICAL TERMS

SALARY: Sailors were paid for their services in part with salt. Salary is a word from the Latin "salaium" meaning "salt". The phrase "worth his salt" means that the sailor is doing a good job. Evidently, I was not worth much to my captains- either in money or salt.

SCUTTLEBUTT: A wooden water cask placed on deck from which sailors could drink, or my pug dragging his butt on the carpet to empty his anal glands.

SHANTY: Songs used by sailors during arduous tasks like weighing anchor, or a tarpaper shack in which we Shanty Irish lived unlike the Lace Curtain Irish who lived in real houses but never to be trusted.

BEAM ENDS: A term used to describe a ship laid over so her beams were underwater, or a picturesque term to describe my wife's tush— before I was hospitalized.

TWENTY-FOUR

NAUTICAL IQ EXAMINATION

The following construct is a test detecting the level of saltiness of the sailor/participant. The answers and norm ratings are at the bottom. The use of calculators, computers, reference material, and the like are prohibited. Wearing of nautical attire, especially a jaunty sailing cap is recommended. Boat shoes are required.

VOCABULARY

Define the following nautical words:

1. Truss

2. Mother Carey's Chicken

3. Mousing

4. Claw

5. Cathead Stopper

6. Feather

NAUTICAL IQ EXAMINATION

7. Galley Staysail

8. Navel Pipe (correct spelling)

9. Reach Ahead

10. Skag

MATH

1. First Rate Ship (number of guns)

2. Hundredweight

3. Number of masts on a Thames wherry

4. Formula for maximum hull speed

5. One (1) meter in fathoms

6. Breaking strength of a quarter inch 3 strand manila line

7. Degrees of all ship's wakes

8. Using international rules, how many horn blasts given when overtaking a vessel on   starboard side

9. Number of feet in a Class A boat (U.S. regulations)

10. Recommended weight of a Danforth anchor for a dinghy under 17 feet

ANSWERS

1. Securing a yard to a mast allowing it to be lowered or raised.

2. Sea Petrel (in plural a slang name for "snow").

3. Rope secured across the opening of a hook to prevent it from clearing itself.

4. Working a vessel to windward from a lee shore to avoid shipwreck.

5. A chain securing an anchor after it has been catted home.

6. To luff a sail so that it catches less wind, used when the wind is too strong or when entering a slip or mooring.

7. Fabric wind scoop used to force air beloved decks for ventilation.

8. Deck fitting though which the anchor passes to the chain locker.

9. The distance traveled between the time an order for new speed is made until the vessel actually attains that speed.

10. Chain on barges thrown over the stern as a drag to attain balance.

1. 100

2. 112 (damn British)

NAUTICAL IQ EXAMINATION

3. 0 (this beast is rowed)

4. S = 1.34 x square root of length at waterline.

5. .55

6. 480 pounds

7. 39 degrees

8. 2 long and 1 short blast

9. Under 16

10. Five (5) pounds

18-20 Correct	Damn Coast Guard Officer; not invited to MY boat party.
16-17	Dork fish, Bo' Suns Mate Chiefs. You bring the beer.
4 - 5	Newbie but tolerable company.
Less than 4 points	You look good in DuBerry's and Nautica. Be sure to wear a boating cap with lots of gold trim or eschew the whole thing and just Messabout for the fun of it.

TWENTY-FIVE

PATRON SAINTS OF WIND, WATER, AND SAILORS

While we may chuckle at the ancient people who had deities they needed to appease for smooth sailing or fair winds; however modern humanity is not too far removed from such considerations. The time of the Vikings or early Egyptians may be long ago, but the elimination of saints during the Protestant Reformation isn't. Catholics and Orthodox Churches still have patron saints to whom prayers are offered for intercession with the Lord God.

In another essay I wrote about Grandma Regan and her absolute devotedness to the Catholic teachings. As mentioned, when we would go out on the river or lake with Uncle Dick, she would be attaching so many medals and scapulars to us that if we ever did end up in the water, we would be so weighed down that we would immediately sink to the bottom. Fortunately, none of ever went over the side. Absolute proof of the manifestation of her prayers, according to her.

The most famous of all Patron Saints of travelers, be it on land, sea, or air, is St. Christopher. The legend of Christopher is that he was a giant

PATRON SAINTS OF WIND, WATER, AND SAILORS

man who dedicated himself to helping people across a raging river or saved many who would have drowned.

St. Christopher was originally honored with a church built in 450 AD during the Council of Chalcedon. Legend has it that he was over 7 feet tall and had a fearsome face. He was aiding the Christians who were being persecuted in Lycia. He was beheaded by a pagan king.

The saintly legend has it that a child asked him to carry him across a river. Then the child identified himself as Jesus, blessed Christopher, and suddenly disappeared. The bureaucrats of the Curia (the Pope's people who run everything Catholic) decided that the current evidence is incomplete and dropped Chris from the calendar of Saint's Days. The Orthodox Church continues to honor him on May 9. St. Justine's Church in Croatia claims that a reliquary holding the saint's skull has been there since 1075. St. Christopher remains an extremely popular saint among the believers.

St. Erasmus (aka St. Elmo as in St. Elmo's fire), is the official patron saint of sailors. His story was that as a religious bishop he comforted persecuted Christians but was killed by an enraged Emperor Diocletian who had Erasmus's bowels pulled out on a windlass. Part of the name issue is that stories often confused him with Erasmus of Antioch. Nevertheless, electrical charges that light up masts and booms during storms were seen as an indication that the ship was safe thanks to St. Elmo.

Being as Irish as Paddy's pig, I prefer St. Brendan, the beloved saint of Ireland who supposedly set forth to the West with other monks to discover and convert. The story has it that he eventually discovered North America long before Columbus. He was born in Fenit, Ireland about 484 and died in Annaghdown in 577. According to my math, that makes him one very old monk. An old Irish immram (books of sea ventures) written around 900, Navigatio Sancti Brendani Abbatis (Voyage of Saint Brendan the Abbot) says that he wandered out to sea in a leather boat. Subsequent experts show that such a boat of that period could, indeed, sail all the way to the Americas.

Actually, flying from Chicago to Helsinki via the Northern route over Greenland, one is amazed at the number of little non-descript islands dotting the route, and it takes no great imagination to think of people moving little-by-little westward. Brendan and Erik could have easily hit the American continent.

St. Nicholas, usually associated as Santa Claus and with Christmas, is a surprisingly Patron Saint of Sailors. Allegedly, the good man was traveling to a new diocese via sea when a storm arose that jeopardized the ship and scared the hell out of the sailors. He quietly took the helm and navigated them to safety. When the sailors later entered a church, they realized that their savior was none other than the Bishop Nicholas. Many old legends are probably apocryphal but this story is realistic and has the ring of truth. Those of us sailors who have indeed been frightened by storms know that someone with a nose for good navigating can actually handle a dangerous situation.

Mary, mother of Jesus, has long been seen as an interceder for people in trouble, especially at sea. In Latin, she is known as *Stella Maris*, Drop of the Sea. Unfortunately, during the manual re-writing or translation of sacred texts, things got a little confusing. In Hebrew, Mary was pronounced *Maryam* but when things got translated into Greek it became Miryam. Eusebius interpreted it as Maryam or drop of the sea. St. Jerome added additional confusion when he translated Stilla Maris as *Stella Maris*, star of the sea.

Anyway, sailors since the earlies ages of Christianity, prayed to Our Lady, Star of the Sea. Of course, it is only natural that Star of the Sea would be associated with the North Star which clerical writers adopted and indicated that when in raging seas, look to the North Star or Star of the Sea and pray to Mary.

PATRON SAINTS OF WIND, WATER, AND SAILORS

For storms and hurricanes, the pious need turn only to St. Medard of France, a 6th century cleric who, as the story goes, was spared of being wet by an eagle who spread his wings over the man. His feast day is 8 June, and, like the Groundhog, if it rains on that day, you will have 40 more days of rain that season.

While not specifically for sailors or for storms, St. Anna, the mother of Mary Mother of Jesus, is seen as a compassionate person that intercedes on behalf of people in trouble. Interestingly, she is also the Patron Saint for unmarried mothers. I suppose they are sailing a troubled sea also.

St. Phocas is a Patron Saint of Gardeners and merchant sailors. Don't ask me why. The story is that a group of Roman soldiers were sent to arrest him. They knocked at a house and were welcomed inside and given a warm welcome. When they discovered that the guy they were to arrest was the host of such great hospitality, they let him go. Like a multitude of saints, he may or may not have actually existed.

If you want a true and glorious story of a saint, you need look no farther than our own American History and Elizabeth Ann Seaton. Her father became a widower after his wife died, possibly in childbirth. He then married Charlotte Barclay, a member of the Jacobus James Roosevelt family. Yes, that Roosevelt family. Charlotte took her stepdaughter, Elizabeth, around to sundry places in New York, tending the poor and doing charitable things. When her father went to Europe on business, Elizabeth and her mother stayed with an uncle, William Bayley, who ensured the upper-class child was tutored in French, art, music, and horsemanship.

At age 19, Elizabeth married William Seton, a prosperous import/export merchant. He was noted for buying and bring the first Stradivarius violin into the United States. Unfortunately, Seton's father's business collapsed during the War of 1812. William took in his six younger siblings including Catherine, who would become the first American to join the Sisters of Mercy.

William died young and his wife and sister eventually lived with Italian business partner, Filippo and Antonio Filicchi. Although a devout member of the Church of England and, after the Revolution, the Episcopalian Church, Elizabeth continued her daily charitable work and care for the sick, dying, and poor. The Filicchi family, being devout Catholics, introduced her to a different religion. She eventually converted to Catholicism.

Working hard for good causes, she helped establish St. Mary's University in Emmitsburg, MD and St. Joseph's School for poor boys. Her upper-crust connections helped her gain the financial support for her endeavors. She founded a religious group in Maryland adopting the rules of the Daughters of Charity. This group is dedicated to charity work among the poor. St. Elizabeth Ann Seton is buried in Emmitsburg. She is the Patron Saint of Seafarers and Widows. She died in 1821 at the age of 46.

In a side bar, Seton's order founded the Bayley Seton hospital on Staten Island, NY, the Mother Seton school in Maryland, Seton Hall College in New Jersey, dozens of Elizabeth Ann Seton high schools, churches, and buildings on the College of Mount Saint Vincent in the Bronx, Niagara University in New York, and Sacred Heart University in Connecticut.

TWENTY-SIX

IOWA WINTER

Iowa was slathered in snow this week. While I should be grateful that we were blessed with an unusually warm autumn allowing only sweatshirts at football games and a light windbreaker at the lake, any time the snow comes at this time of year it will remain until April, and my water experience is over for the season. It also signals the onset of my chronic depression, acute anxiety, and general irascibility. My shrink, a salubrious and arrogant snob complete with disgustingly handsome looks, thick blonde hair, brilliant mind, and a smell of money says, "Get a job, swallow some pills, avoid wintery days, and take an expensive vacation". This takes 3 minutes. He charges me $180 so he can take long weekends in the Bahamas. I should find a job?! What the hell would he know about work?

My doctorate in psychology proffers a different perspective than my shrink: go south, take the boat, take the dog, and leave the wife at home. I have an intuitive belief that my depression, seasonal attitude disorder (which no doubt commenced when they started blaring Christmas music at the mall three days before Halloween), and general malaise will disappear immediately upon the sight of salt water, beat up old boat yards, or even a rippling lake sparkling in the sunshine

"Messing About In Boats" takes on a more medicinal interest to me during the winter. During the rest of the year, it offers many interesting articles, some Robb Smith's quiet and soothing discourses, enviable photos of boats built by significantly more talented people than me, and a plethora of ads with Internet addresses that I can view at my leisure when I can't sleep at night. During winter, *MAIB* becomes my only connection with sanity. I also absorb Ken Murphy's SHALLOW WATER SAILOR, which is way too short, comes way too infrequently, and is way too good to not sit down and devour immediately at the closest chair next to the mail slot. Eight pages aren't enough to cut my boat withdrawal symptoms but neither is *MAIB, SAIL, L&A, GOOD OLD BOAT, SMALL BOAT ADVISOR, WOODEN BOAT*, and a smattering of others that come too seldom to meet my privation.

Catalogs are OK since I can and do review them daily and too often buy unimportant "stuff" just to await nautical materials coming in the mail. Waiting for the mail is about the only fun thing in an Iowa winter.

Everyone around here knows that I possess a doctorate and thus assume I am a total idiot and eccentric. Plumbers love my Do-It-Yourself projects around the house almost as much as car mechanics. Carver ACE hardware gives my all sorts of little gifts like key chains and coffee mugs since I am their Ace customer. Each clerk recognizes me immediately during the winter since my withdrawal symptoms are somewhat mitigated by sauntering around in naval attire from my sea bag. I have acquired a wool Greek fisherman's hat to keep my balding pate warm, a plethora of U.S. Navy caps from various ships I have visited or given by veteran crews whom I have addressed (sometimes I actually get money for my blathering and blarney), and an old pea coat. I have a silly yachtsman cap for wearing around the house as I pretend that I actually command this home and my dog and cat are loyal seamen. I am convinced that wearing some sort of water clothing is a necessity when reading my magazines during the winter. Hey, I consider my malady serious in nature and it requires significant psychological adjustment.

The Christmas season struck with a mighty blow complete with the usual smatterings of trampling at Wal-Mart, a couple of Salvation Army Santas making off with the pot, a multitude of Ho Ho Hos from ordinarily decent businessmen who imbibed too many Tom and Jerry. Son, Timothy, knows what dad needs and deserves for presents: gift cards to Barnes and Noble. Barnes and Noble, usually reliable for offering decent books for a plethora of divergent folks, have stripped the aisles and shelves of anything resembling sailing, water, boats, knots, and such, and these have been replaced by a pile of gifts; books for silly people to spend large sums of money on to give to equally silly people who shall never read the leather-bound version of **War and Peace**. I did find a paperback version of **Maiden Voyage**. I bought it before they shunted it away to the nether world of the back room.

As aforementioned, I vehemently disagree with the psychiatrist. I think I should continue the pills, skip the job part, and avoid winter entirely by saving my shrink money and sailing in the Caribbean from December to April of each and every year. While I have no empirical data to support my contention, I do believe that sailing is pretty much a cure-all for most maladies including those with aqua phobia (a little salt water and facing the fear directly is a wonderful idea). In fact, on additional contemplation, I believe there is a professional research article being born here. I should take my current psychological depression that arrives promptly on November First and fails to leave until the boat is launched in early April and use the number of times my Miss I Love Frozen Finland 1953 threatens me with murder if I don't lighten up as the base line. The experiment would be to take my seasonally attitude depressed body and place it for approximately one month in some warmer climate where I can scuba dive and sail to my heart's content. Cozumel would be appropriate, Hawaii is beyond my financial reach, and Bali or Pago Pago is more of a dream.

My research article would be "The Impact of Winter Sailing in the Tropics on Seasonal Attitude Disorder" and it would be complete with graphs and lots of statistical stuff subscribing to a notion that is as obvious as the nose on your face; but that is what social research is all about. Toss a t-test or an Analysis of Variance in somewhere. Whether the data supports the hypothesis is irrelevant just as long as it is "almost" significant, which to a statistician is like being almost pregnant: either you is or you ain't. But most people don't know statistics worth a damn, so lots of graphs and numbers impresses the hell out of them. I have served on the editorial board of several professional psychology journals so I know that writing in the passive voice, using lots of big words, showing tons of graphs and statistics will make the article reviewable. If it is so darn complicated that no one could possibly understand it I guarantee it will be published because no editor would admit they didn't have a clue about what the article was saying. Being very long and boring is also a positive trait for professional journals.

Currently the topic of spirituality in psychology is hot. If I play my cards right, I can also toss in a variable about finding God on a sailboat during winter while I sailing with a bikini clad buxom stewardess named Bambi. That will get the article published for sure. AND I might even have to present the findings at some American Psychological Association or American Counseling Association conference, preferably in a nice warm climate during the following winter. I actually did slap together some stuff on suicides in schools for the ACA conference in San Diego a few years back. The conference was in early March. Iowa had a snowstorm. I got sunburn on the beach...whoops, I just gave away the secret that I didn't attend a whole lot of other sessions at the conference.

The more that I contemplate this research the more I am convinced that it is worthy of a substantial grant from some obscure entity that funds ludicrous research like the profound study that showed that left-handed teachers use more prepositions than right-handed teachers, information that certainly changed my life drastically, especially since I don't know a preposition from a gerund. There just must be some organization that will finance my endeavors from early November until late Spring

Until Bill Gates forks over the moola or I win the Powerball Lottery, I will just play with the contemptible snow blower, take long naps with the pug, and generally hibernate. Benjamin Franklin said, " Beer is proof that God loves us and wants us to be happy". Doc Regan says, "Tom and Jerrys" are proof that God loves us and wants us to become oblivious to winter.

TWENTY-SEVEN

KNIVES

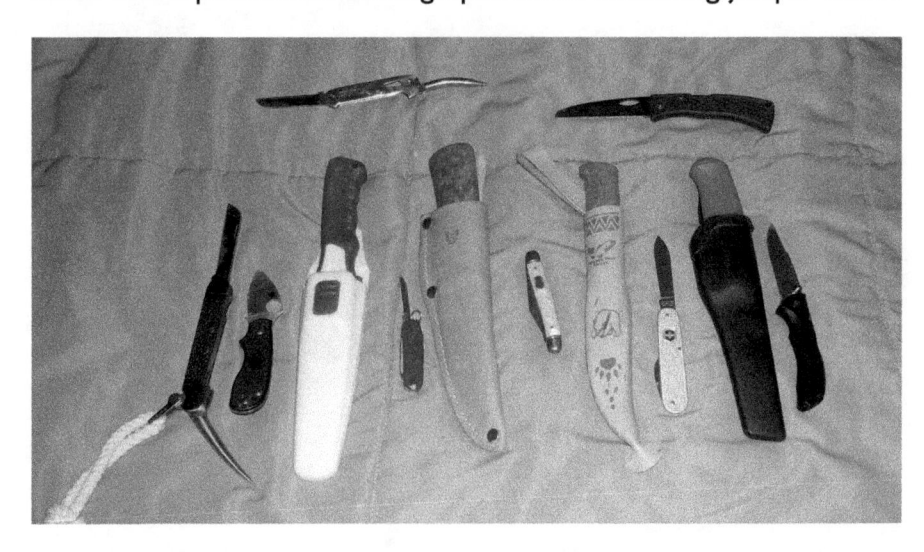

From my earliest days in teacher education classes I gleaned that certain students ranging from kindergarten to graduate school should never be around sharp objects because they may hurt themselves or others accidentally or on purpose. In my innocence I thought that the biggest problem was little tykes running with scissors; but I was wrong. Big kids do stupid things with sharp objects too. I won't mention the useless tip of the middle finger on my left hand after I severed the nerve with a pocketknife cutting open a box containing jumper cables after I left my lights on all night.

What really bothers me is that carrying a knife of any size is a MANDATORY 1-year expulsion from school in Iowa. Of course, every farm kid in the state has a pocketknife on him; but the damn get-tough-on-crime folks decided that 1 Strike and you're out is absolute! I won't even talk about what would happen if you tried to board a plane with a blade on your finger nail clippers. Nor will I mention the time that I tried to board a plane in Mexico but had forgotten my dive knife in my brief case. Believe me, the Mexican police are a whole lot nicer than the Cedar Rapids, Iowa, police. They just laughed at me and made me stow it in my luggage. The C.R. cops would have fired automatic assault weapons first and asked questions later.

I do not recall a time I did not have a little jack knife in my pocket. How else would a boy sharpen his pencil, play Stretch, cut string, carve his name in his school desk, nip the wick on the altar candles, or cut the Irish Pennants from his altar boy cassock? God only knows when and where I got my first knife but I am sure that somewhere along the line my beloved grandfather, Feats, gave me one when I was about 5 years old. I have possessed a plethora of them since then and remarkably, many of them are still around the house in sundry drawers. I still have one from grade school, one of Feats's pocketknives that I gave to my son, a nice small knife, a little Swiss do-everything knife that is my day-to-day choice, and a smattering of others collected along the way.

Talking about knives to small boaters is a bit like talking about toothpaste: it is an essential ingredient for life. Lines need to be sliced, string needs to be severed, tubing needs to be cut, plastic wrap needs removing, crap needs to be chipped, wood needs to be whittled. Duh! A sailor without a knife is like an old retired college dean and inverted boater without a beer.

The rationale for this little epistle is that I spent the week end cleaning up odds and ends on my little Boatex 1200 sailboat and my mammoth 12-foot Boston Whaler. The former needed new lines and some additional "stuff" added. The latter needed a newer gas line, a new pull rope for the motor, a new electrical line to the lights, and some new stuff, I ended up laughing at myself because when Miss Unnaslahti, Frigid Maiden of the Finns, returned and started yelling about all the junk all over the driveway I looked over my collection of screw drivers, wrenches, and knives scattered all over the place and realized I am a tool-aholic. I had no fewer than 4 knives laid out for various service: a small one for getting into tight spots, a larger one for bigger jobs, a box cutter to open the containers of "stuff" and an extra one when I couldn't reach any of the others. Only a true sailor would understand the absolute need for at least 4 knives when working on a boat.

On a lark, I started to get my knife collection in some sort of grouping ranging from small dress knives to large, kill sharks type of blades. Perhaps my favorite is the handmade Heimo Roselli blade that Mr. Roselli made from scratch at his home in Finland about 8 miles from my father-in-law's place. Roselli knives may be purchased in the U.S. for upwards of $170. Mine was a present from Miss Nordic Fling's eldest brother, Ari Unnaslahti, and he paid a lot less. The blade itself is high carbon steel beaten and folded for ages on end from ore collected from the rocks at Heimo's cabin, the scabbard is leather which he sewed up as we were waiting around the barn, the birch handle came from one of his millions of birches behind the house. This is a real knife: plain, simple, keen, and rugged in the usual Finnish design with short blade and long handle minus a finger guard. You skin bear and moose with these things.

My other Finnish knife is a wonderful Fiskers with a plastic handle. It is the el cheapo of work knives. Again, with a high carbon steel blade, this little shaver is razor sharp, dirt cheap, and in every Finn's fishing equipment. I bought a bundle of these for presents to the delinquents in my neighborhood. The other Finnish knife is a Rapala hunting knife that I purchased for a lot of Finn Marks only to discover they are cheaper at Wal-Mart on Blair's Ferry Road.

My dive knife is blunt ended supposedly useful in prying open stuff, oyster shells or popping the top off Mexican beer bottles. Of course, all divers worth their air need to be decorated with a dive knife that they never, ever use. They are handy forgettable tools in one's carry-on luggage. Ask any experienced diver; they have all been caught boarding planes with a dive knife. One truly has to wonder if any diver has actually used their knife or do they all just wear one for show. Hmmmm

The easy one-handed flip knives are handy dandy items around the boat. I keep a larger one on each boat for sundry purposes like cutting myself free of entangled lines. A smaller version is a pocket sample to be used in time of great distress like when I am trapped under water in a concoction of ropes and wires and general stuff when I attempt my stunt of inverted sailing.

I do not think this is the time or place to mention that once upon a time my beloved Feats took brother Mikey and me across the border to Reynosa Mexico. Mikey wanted a knife so the elderly dentist took the 6th grader to a knife shop and found a "cute" little thing for the boy. It was a switchblade. Mike took it to St. Patrick's elementary school and sold it for a fortune.

Maybe that's why Mikey is rich and I am still a fiscal burden on my wife and children.

TWENTY-EIGHT

BOAT DOGS

Articles of sundry nautical subjects appear by the boatload in the various magazines and newsletters that we all receive and patiently read immediately upon arrival; however, evidence show a paucity of boat and dog related comments. See a flotilla of boats and see a yelping pack of canines. Man, beast, and boat seem to be the universal requirement for happiness around water. Those of us who look for women and beer as the source of all things good are sadly mistaken.

Canines have always been the subjects of keen interest partially because they seem so loyal and fun but also because there are many varieties of them. Movies run the gamut from the Cairn terrier of *Wizard of Oz* to the Collie brilliance of *Lassie* to German Sheppard *Rin Tin Tin*. No one can forget Frank, the Pug who leads *the Men in Black*. Unfortunately, the movies of boats and boaters seem to have porpoises, behemoth whales, or cartoon fish but we don't see curs and cruising a silver screen match. Marinas, on the other hand, are home to a plethora of pooches.

A number of Animal Planet or National Geographic TV shows have featured our beloved mutts noting that: a) dogs are but recent descendants of wolves, b) they have understood that a close mutual relationship with homo sapiens is a good thing c) they come in more varieties than all us MAIB readers can count on our fingers and toes. Together we share food and love in exchange for protection and affection. This seems to be a better deal than many marriages.

One reason for the incredible variety of breeds is that canines possess a "slippery" gene that allows significant changes in the appearance of the dog within a generation or two. One research project started with wild wolf and raised it in the lab. Within a single generation the wolf offspring were more approachable, had less smelling capabilities, were smaller, less easily startled, and had a smoother coat. Within a couple of generations, the subjects were far more akin to Sheppard's than to wolves. Think about it, within about 12,000 years wolves became Pugs, Pekinese, Newfoundlands, Cardigan Welsh Corgi, Chihuahuas, Mastiffs, etc. Modern dogs range from the very large to the incredibly small, from weird hair to hairless, from lap dogs to scent dogs. Pooches come in almost two hundred recognized varieties to say naught of the mutts or designer dogs.

With all the hoopla of the Westminster Dog Show and the Animal Planet, time has come to look at some boating type dogs. Many breeds are excellent water/boating types; but many breeds are definitely not sailors. Admittedly a dog of a certain type will be an excellent boater in spite of the evidence to the contrary, and others will be deathly afraid of water despite being a water-oriented breed. It is about the same with people.

Many of the Sporting dog division are excellent around water. Spaniels, Retrievers, Newfoundlands, Poodles, Portuguese Water Dogs, and Schipperkes are well known for their love of water. Put a Black Lab near water and you can play fetch for a day without a respite. The Newfoundland was an accidental water dog supposedly evolved from various dogs that swam ashore from shipwrecks. Clearly Mastiff, St. Bernard, and other large dogs were among its ancestors. Newfies are natural water retrievers who will by nature swim out to a person in trouble on the water.

But most canines are land dogs and prefer solid ground underfoot. Sheppards and terriers hunters are woodsy animals. Pugs, small terriers, hairy Asian dogs like the Pekinese and Shih Tzu tend to be very happy curled up in a person's lap in front of the fireplace.

If a boating person were to look for a dog, one should consider each breed's characteristics as it pertains to their domicile, recreation habits, and children or grandchildren. In spite of many arguments to the contrary specific breeds are very owner oriented and can be difficult around visitors, especially children. The guard-type dogs and pit bulls are not good around people other than their owners. Again, some of them are excellent around children or strangers but the exceptions are very rare. A quick trip to the animal shelters in your community will show that the numerous pit bull or pit bull types are there because people thought it was cool to own them but discovered they were unable to handle them.

Lap dogs, by and large (a nautical term in itself), tend to be less than happy on boats unless it is a large boat like a houseboat or pontoon boat. Pugs do not jump for joy at the thought of being on the water and most of their smaller buddies are similar. For one thing, many of the smaller breeds are flat-faced which creates a breathing problem for them. They do not handle heat (or cold) particularly well because they cannot cool off fast enough and they become stressed. Worse, these little tidbits and fur balls are so darn loyal that they will not complain until they are in serious trouble.

Many water dogs are great retrievers but that too comes with a cost. Several varieties have waterproof coats that are oily. This means that they will leave dirty spots on furniture, rugs, and upholstery. The oils will also proffer a "doggy" smell when they are wet. Anybody that has been around dogs knows that "wet dog" aroma. Many of these dogs are also large and can be intimidating to visitors and children. A large Chesapeake Bay retriever jumping up on you can scare the daylights out of anyone. They also are good scent dogs and crotch sniffing is a given.

There is something to the rule of thumb that says the bigger the dog the more friendly the dog. While I don't care what the rule states when it comes to pit bulls, I must agree that big monsters like the Newfoundland and Saint Bernard certainly correlate with it. Newfies are perhaps the best of the best for being around water. Huge, easy with children and strangers, intelligent, the Newfoundland will soften the hardest of hearts. The St Bernard also falls into this category but my personal experience with the St Bernard has not been overly wonderful. My fraternity had one. The behemoth was dim witted, boisterous, virtually untrainable, and well known for his ability to knock down people chiefly people who do not like being knocked down and whom we did not want being knocked down, i.e., university presidents, deans, parents, elderly alumni. I refuse to believe that the dog's social failures were linked to our Brotherly ineptness as trainers, consistent disciplinarians, or our own social behaviors (read that "Animal House").

Another rule of thumb is that the larger the dog the shorter the life span. Wonderful old wooly Newfies are about ten when they hit the upper limits of the age scale. For many people that is just too short for such a wonderful animal. Yappy little fur balls ostensibly bred to be winter muffs for elderly ladies can live long, long lives. My neighbor's little chronic barker must be at least 30. It certainly seems that way because no one can remember not hearing that constant barking.

I know of many varieties make good boat companions. Observing marinas, messabouts, and nautical gatherings, I have seen just about every kind of mutt enjoying their day on the water. One neighbor couple spent their entire summers on their boat that their beloved schnauzer enjoyed as much as the humans. Another pontoon dweller's Schipperke was purchased precisely because their love of water matched the couple's; unfortunately, the dog was fiercely protective and anyone else boarding the boat had to be examined, re-examined, and passed reluctantly before the offending person was allowed near the vessel. Schipperkes (Dutch for "little skipper") are born to be on a deck. From the earliest of their history, they stood in weather fair and foul at the feet of their captains at the helm. Loyal and beloved by their human partners, the Schipperke is not particularly friendly with other dogs or anyone other than the crew.

Admiral Frank Jack Fletcher, WWII Coral Sea and Midway commander, always had a fondness for dogs. One photo shows him with his dog boringly hosting Russian officers during a Lend-Lease meeting. His French bulldog during World War I was a dirty, foul-smelling mutt that universally was detested. When it accidently fell overboard in harbor the crew argued mightily about whether to save the mascot. Only because of the crew's admiration for Fletcher was the dog rescued. "Pouli" might have been hated but he remains a topic of Fletcher lore, and has been cited in sundry historical articles and books including

Fletcher's biography written by naval historian Dr. Stephen D. Regan.

Fletcher's Alaskan pet became a victim of the press when it was reported by Republican oriented writers that President Roosevelt had sent a destroyer from the Pacific war zone to retrieve his pet Scottish Terrier. Actually, his little dog was accidently left at North Pacific Fleet headquarters with Fletcher's dog instead of being transported with the President's luggage to the U.S.S. Baltimore for transport to California. A young officer retrieved the First Mutt and brought him to the harbor. Little Fala was loved by the Commander in Chief but he was also a good little sailor onboard a Navy cruiser.

On a very personal note, I must admit that my boating love and my best pal ever are totally inappropriate. Spencer the Perfect Pug demands he go everywhere I go but is notoriously known to let me know that my little West Wight Potter 15 is about 60 feet too small for his liking and its propensity for heeling is equally unacceptable. My little buddy needs to be forcibly moved from the wonderful solidness of the dock to the miserable deck. He lies at me feet whimpering during the entire trip unless we start the motor at which he insists on howling at. (Whoever heard of a pug howling!) When we get within six feet of the dock, he does a puggy type long jump toward shore. Yet, if I should leave him at the dock with my wife he cries until I come get him. If it is warm, he refuses to go into the cabin from which he lets me know will suddenly collapse around him or will trap him when we sink, and sink we surely shall. He also exhibits his displeasure by wrapping any lines available around himself ensuring both a trend for the captain to fall on his face or botch any movement that is required to make the sail safe. Worse, his hatred of the boat and demand to go along with me on it has been consistent for ten summers. Spencer the Perfect Pug is the best dog in the world but the worst sailor on the planet. No wonder cruising is not in the cards for me.

Again, dogs on a boat are ubiquitous. When selecting a breed, sailors should be mindful of their habits, recreation, entertainment, and behavior and pick a dog that correlates well. A Newfoundland is a wonderful water dog but it is pretty darn big for a Potter 15. On the other hand, a greyhound is likely to be problematic on a yacht. But if you already have a dog and want to make it more water-friendly, you have some heavy training and acquainting to do. (Whoever heard of a pug howling!).

TWENTY-NINE

SPRINGTIME FOR STUPID STEVE

The sun shines and the wind blows which, translated into the King's English, means that it is time to rouse myself from the mental hibernation of the winter and prepare for a summer of sailing. As robins swoop in from the South and deposit their excrements all over my boat, I find myself thinking diligently about the previous boat season and the multitude errors of judgment, decisions of stupidity, and the plethora of problems promulgated by perturbingly poor reasoning.

Last fall in a lapse of intelligence, I decided on one last sail across the lake. Unfortunately, the wind was brisk, very brisk and the park staff was in preparation of taking in the docks. But Dummy Doc launched anyway. I motored into the middle of the lake and promptly commenced to raise sail (I discovered that raising sail at the dock usually ends up swamping, capsizing, or being pushed against the rocks). Of course, the sail refused to go up the mast because of a jam. Being incredibly stupid, I took down the mast and tried to fix the problem. Meanwhile the boat was rapidly pushed across the lake toward the lee shore. I suddenly realized the problem and started the motor only to have the fuel line connection break and I ended up on the rocks.

To add to my misery, I could not get off the rocks nor do much of anything since I was jammed tightly. Where are fishermen when you need them? Certainly not out on the lake when the wind is whooping up large whitecaps and foam. A gathering of Harley Davidson types complete with beards and leathers wandered by and offered assistance to one so mentally challenged as me. We finally managed the boat toward the landing only to discover that the docks had been removed by previously mentioned park personnel. OK, so now my next spring preparation includes a serious touch-up of scrapped hull.

In my educational career I was pleased to learn about various intelligences. Some of us have modest mathematical-logical reasoning and reading ability so we score high on standard IQ tests. Unfortunately, those IQ tests (still often required by many states) fail to consider the myriad of other intelligences such as musical ability. I may have a very high IQ but never could play the piano or guitar worth spit while others seem to pick up musical talent like I pick up colds. I was trained as a linguist for the Defense Department and am proud to admit I was the worst student in the history of the Defense Language Institute. My silly roommate not only studied German and Spanish in college, he was trained in Arabic by the Navy and ended up a better French speaker than I did merely listening to my tapes. Another acquaintance speaks 8 languages fluently and probably another six or seven adequately to get by on a vacation. This is innate intelligence not shown on IQ tests.

My neighbor Mike is a genius unparalleled. He can fix anything. He understands how things work and can foresee issues well in advance of the problem. He knows tools and how to use them. I call on him weekly for assistance. I didn't even know that there are dozens of different types of wrenches nor know that a tack hammer, a ball peen hammer, and a regular hammer are different devices for different uses. Please do not ask what they are for other than hammering stuff. Neighbor Mike is brilliant; I am severely and profoundly mechanically challenged.

So now I come to my spring boating duties. First, I need a topping lift because it will help me raise the sails a lot easier. Believe me I was proud to admit that I made one after three trips to Ace Hardware and two days of messing around. Other than sticking my mast through a window, the need for a couple of stitches, and a handful of splinters, it was accomplished.

I need an adequate mast crutch. You know, one that actually works. After designing and planning several models, I have discovered that no matter what I build, it will fall over with minimal enticement. And Iowa's roads and potholes are more than amply enticing. I even tried making one of several free weights that would not slide around or tip over only to hit a small bump and have 25-pound weights flying all over the place at windshield high levels. Clearly, my ability to see, to anticipate, and prepare for such endeavors is far beyond my mental capacity. Books I can write, degrees I have attained, leadership I can provide but a simple freaking mast crutch is so far beyond my scope of knowledge it frightens me.

Raising a mast is, unto itself, a rigorous task. I have developed a simple device that uses an old winch from a previously destroyed boat trailer. Naturally, trying to attach this to my new trailer has created months and months of planning, designing, sawing, wiring, taping, pounding, welding, gluing, and prayer. Even with a Novena to St. Erasmus and St. Christopher, I can't get the darn thing to work consistently. It seems so simple. I am too ashamed to turn to Neighbor Mike who will fix this thing correctly and to perfection in 3 minutes. I will fight with it all year.

In the aftermath of my lee shore adventure last fall I managed to rip out a cleat. I realize that the cleat was, evidently, held in place by two screws drilled into the fiberglass. The fiberglass is about 1/16th of an inch in thickness and won't hold anything. Worse, the place where the cleat resided is unreachable from underneath. First, I tried filling up the holes with about 2 gallons of epoxy. This was futile. I tried little plastic inserts that worked wonderfully until there was any semblance of pressure and then they disappeared into the ethers.

An Internet associate with sailing experiences suggested drilling a large hole, using a backing plate, and repairing the hole with a deck plate. Somehow, the thought of drilling a large hole in my boat scares the hell out of me. I may try it.

First, let me check my life insurance and AFLAC. How can one with four college degrees be so incredibly mechanically incompetent?? Maybe Neighbor Mike will help in exchange for a six-pack of Miller Light or Corona. Light a candle for me until then.

THIRTY

Good Old Finnish Row Boat

No country enjoys as many lakes as Finland, which rightly claims over 80,000 not counting small little lakes that more often as not are not even named. This Land of the Midnight Sun boasts 24 hours of sunlight at Midsummer's Night but has incredibly lengthy daylight most of the summer (of course, in winter the sun hardly rises over the forests and then for a brief spell). The Finns have lake water in their veins; virtually all families have a cabin or access to a cabin in the dense pine forests beside a lake. Suomi, the Finnish name for their country, allows a minimum of four weeks' vacation which is usually taken in July, and this Nordic country's populace will be on or near water both oceanic or lake all summer.

The Finns are an ancient people who have inhabited the region for thousands of years. Early Romans mentioned "Fenns" who lived in the North. Neither Scandinavian nor Slavic, they are an anthropological oddity as is their language. Their body structure of long, broad faces and high foreheads, and brown hair is unlike their Swedish and Norwegian neighbors and a quite distinct from the Russians with whom they share an 800-mile border. Their language is astonishingly different from all other languages except Sami, Karelian and Estonian although there is some remote and virtually unidentifiable relationship to Hungarian.

Because of their ancient history and watery home, the Finns are definitely water people who have lived along the lakes and used the water as an inherent element of their livelihood. Fish, wood and paper products were their largest industry until the formation of Nokia and the development of new computer operating systems.

A quick purview of the map of Finland notes that about one third of the country is above the Arctic Circle and sparsely inhabited. The lower two-thirds are basically lakes separated with a little land that make Minnesota look like a desert. It is almost a rite of adulthood to have a piece of land given or sold to an offspring on which they can build their cabins. In my case, Kalevi Unnaslahti has built houses or cabins at each of the three lakes that border his farm for his four sons and one that is semi-designated for his daughter, my wife. Therefore, we are blessed at seeing a myriad of Finns plying the waves seeking fish.

Having spent parts of three summers in Finland, I know that virtually every Finn has a sauna, a Nokia cell phone, and a nice old rowboat. Fish continues to be a main element of the Finnish diet, and especially in the rural areas, the process of netting or catching fish is as primary to these people as breathing, saunas, and vodka.

Because of the daylight, such comments as the "crack of dawn" means nothing. I have fished in sunlight at midnight! But Finns launch each morning to set nets and again at night to see what they caught. While fishing is a wonderful pastime, the required fish for food greatly surpasses what a hook and line can proffer. They tend to use gill nets to obtain whitefish, perch, and an occasional pike (which they generally consider both the Northern and the Muskie). A bony little fish called Sarki is too small for eating but provide bait, food for gulls, and treats for the omnipresent cat.

Papa Unnaslahti's rowboat is intriguing not because it is unique or unusual, but rather the opposite: it was typical and common. It looks so much like thousands of others from Jyvaskyla to Helsinki that it must be considered a characteristically Finnish boat. Like its peers, the boat is out in the morning and again at night.

The Unnaslahti rowboat was built in Sysma. The "Loki" is approximately 12 feet long with a generous five-foot plus beam (understand that I am vaguely changing metric to English measurements). This fiberglass beauty is built with a broad, flat bottom that delivers an almost non-existent draft. Two sets of oarlocks allow the boat to be rowed both forward and backward and from different vantage points. The Loki has a series of footholds that supports greater leverage for rowing in any position. With its width and length, it can handle about as many adults as you want or as much fishing equipment as you can pile aboard with alacrity.

One of the weak points of the boat is that it is not easily navigated with improper distribution of weight. With my wife sitting at the bow and me forward rowing, it was like trying to paddle a teacup. Moving her to the rear made all the difference. I prefer to row backwards from the rear with any fishing equipment up front; my brother-in-law likes sitting up front with the gear abaft. Either way works fine as seen in the accompanying photos. All steering problems disappear quickly due to inertia. Once moving it plows a straight furrow through the water.

Homemade oars that extend well over the 8-foot mark make this boat incredibly speedy. A few boats fiddle around with small engines of the 4 hp category but the Unnaslahti family, like most Finns, would rather use manual labor. With the protracted oars and shallow draft, the Loki can develop a speed not too far from the powered models. As a dinghy sailor, I was jealous of the speed Loki could suggest.

Any small craft lover will immediately be infatuated with Finland and her lakes. Seeing the myriad of rowboats will entice you to clamber aboard and work some muscles. For those not into fishing or uninterested in the sights, a nice Grillilenkki (sausage) fried over a campfire on one of the islands (dried wood and pine needles are gathered within easy reach anywhere) and a good cold Koff beer before the evening sauna is as close to heaven as it gets.

THIRTY-ONE

SPECIAL REPORT FROM THE U.S. NAVY

As president of the Cedar Rapids chapter of the Navy League, I receive a plethora of Navy journals, magazine, and other information. The most recent edition of SEAPOWER contained a revelation of technology and science recently discovered by the finest naval engineers in response to the declining budgetary support for naval ships.

Some readers may have served in the Coast Guard or the Navy and know that steel hulls and salt water make a miserable match. Ships constantly need scrapping and painting to lessen damage from rust as every photo of a Navy ship notes. Not only are those rust streaks uncomely, they are destructive. Every newbie seaman has enjoyed the pleasure of scrapping and painting in the time-consuming maintenance of hulls. Furthermore, steel ships are notoriously weighty. The current construction consists of modules that are so difficult to move only a few sites in America can transfer hull sections in spite of the easy on-easy off concept of marine building.

Among the recent attempts to develop better, lighter ship requiring less maintenance the Navy used aluminum or even titanium ships.

Unfortunately, as seen on the USS STARK, aluminum burns easily. Aluminum and titanium are fairly expensive vis-à-vis steel; therefore, the finest of MIT, Cal Tech, and civilian ship builders' engineers searched for newer concepts.

With great bravado and limitless enthusiasm, the Navy issued its Special Report on maintenance-free hulls. In the March 2012 issue of SEAPOWER, the Navy and Huntington-Ingalls Industries stated that they "discovered" VARTM or Vacuum Assisted Resin Transfer Molding.

"We place layers of carbon fiber material over the balsa wood core, then seal with a plastic vacuum bag connected to the resin system. When we evacuate all the air and pull a vacuum on the bag, it draws the resin in." said director of fabrication Jay Jenkins of HII. With composite hulls, there is no rust; therefore, crews can be smaller and concentrate on warfare without spending precious time and energy on maintenance.

Wow. I almost jumped out of my skin with excitement. How have we managed without this "modern" technology? Should we be publishing this new technology in public journals? No doubt scores of MIT Ph.D.s, Cal Tech engineers, and naval architects spent immeasurable hours generating this system. Unfortunately, most readers of POPULAR SCIENCE were using that to make rowboats, canoes, and little sailboats a half century ago.

As a sailor of a small craft, I have been using balsa and epoxy for years to repair my occasional mishaps such as smacking into rocks, jetties, docks, and other boats. After my first two major holes which cost me significant sums that I did not have floating around -- actually my billfold was at the bottom of the lake, I learned how to mix epoxy resins and mold stuff myself. Interestingly it was about 10 years ago. Gee just think what a help I would be to the Navy research and development. Unfortunately, when I was in Uncle Sam's Canoe Club, they

SPECIAL REPORT FROM THE U.S. NAVY

just plopped me behind a desk facing mountains of encrypted communications and told me to solve them. After four years of reading the Washington Post and doing crossword puzzles and breaking not a single message, they awarded me a Letter of Commendation and a discharge. Boy oh Boy, did they miss what I had to offer. I could have designed all sorts of new hull models based on the minds of the greatest naval warfare architects such as Dynamite Payson, Mississippi Bob Brown, and Jim Michalak.

Robb White could have developed a new Littoral Combat ship or Joint High Speed Vessel with such ease and cost reduction that we would not have the current economic debt crisis. Heck, I bet he could have built such ships on the beach in half the time Ingalls could in their massive shipyard. West Marine would have been our primary materials support, Hamilton Marine could be our back up, and manuals could be from **MAIB** and **Latitudes and Attitudes**. Put Dan Rogers at the helm and C. Henry Depew as Officer in charge of ship preservation and then we could tell our Arab friends to keep their oil.

Naval Engineers!? I am surprised we have evolved beyond the **USS MONITOR** or **USS MARGARET**.

THIRTY-TWO

Small Craft for Thinkers

Small craft sailing is one of those endeavors made especially for thinkers. Any old dolt with a splash of intelligence can operate a motorboat, albeit operating a motorboat and intelligence is rarely used in the same sentence. By and large (a nautical phrase I happen to use often), you just have to push a button, shove off, and steer. Evidently, consumption of large quantities of alcohol is a requisite in most states. No real thought is put into such an activity. But try sailing near a trio of motor boater beer guzzling, half conscious, blind to the people, places and things around them, and the sailor will end up in deep and probably expensive pooh.

Nope, sailing takes brains and concentration, and yet we still make a plethora of mistakes, screw ups, and goofs. Sailing is complicated and takes thinking, planning, and knowledge. Any neophyte can jump in a motorboat with absolutely no prior training, comprehension, understanding, or knowledge and probably do just fine -- certainly at the level of the average boater and significantly higher than many.

I used to own a nice little Boston Whaler with a 25-horse power motor that got me around where I wanted to go. Of course, I could never go the speed of the rest of the maniacs in the Cedar or Mississippi river, but I could be pleasantly happy. My wife loved the little boat because she had more confidence with a motor than with a sail. It was a rather unique little boat and we got many compliments. But I had my Potter, a canoe, my Whaler, and a little Boatex 12. My lawn began to look like a boatyard and the neighbors complained. Not that we live in a ritzy suburb but we do live across the street from a small college, and we are surrounded by quaint professors, attorneys, and an occasional man of the cloth. They prefer hydrangea bushes and rose gardens with well-manicured lawns that only heavy dosages of chemicals can produce. Captain Pappy Yoakum Regan with his boats, buckets, lines, anchors, and other accoutrements lying around the property is not up to their taste.

The Boatex went to Edina, MN (you do not move to Edina; you achieve Edina!). The little Whaler was left sorrowfully in St. Paul with a nice businessman who wanted something to putter around with his little grandchildren. The canoe surprisingly disappeared on the top of one of my wife's friend's car. Ms. Finland stood smiling broadly with a couple of hundred bucks in her hand. That reminds me, just where did that money for MY canoe go?

Those pitiful souls who only have a motorboat spend a significant level of money on gas. One friend said that a typical day on the Mississippi cost him about $50 in gas to say naught about beer, brats, and miscellaneous munchies. I can hit the lake with a bottle of tap water. No question about it, sailing is costly. One, you always need something. Two, you cannot enter a marine store without purchasing something. Three, you always have some sort of silly idea about how to make your sailing more easy, more efficient, more comfortable, more something. Unfortunately, this is a drawback for us who think! Sailors always are thinking, and they are usually thinking about boats.

As a scholar (well, Mississippi Bob might challenge that concept), I spend a sizeable quantum of time on philosophical questions, cosmology, etymology, epistemology, theology, history, and sociology. Sailing provides a wonderful opportunity to engage oneself in such endeavors. Amazingly, many of the world's problems have been solved within the hemispheres of my brain. If only someone would listen.

A friend of mine has a bumper sticker that reads, "Agnostic: I don't know and you don't either!" As a practicing Catholic (I practice once or twice a year), I have spent legendary amounts of time in courses studying New and Old Testament, Christian history, theology, and Christology. The more I study, the more I think. I have been taking a take-home course on Quantum Mechanics. I listen to a lecture and then have to cogitate for a couple of weeks trying to comprehend a mere fraction of the information. If there is anything to quantum physics at all, then God must be far, far beyond our comprehension. One day meditating on my little **GENNY SEA,** I decided that I probably would not go to hell for eating meat on a Friday when I was a kid. And my elderly mother won't go to hell because she belongs to the United Church of Christ. Maybe (God forbid) those nuns were not particularly right on everything (although if you challenged one of the VEILS you got smacked). Quantum physics and theology: a couple of good days of sailing.

One day, many years ago, an excellent mathematics teacher decided to allow a free day for general classroom discussion on any pertinent topic. He did make one rule: no talking about sex, religion, or politics. One delightful and obviously brilliant student to say nothing of his good looks and radiant personality, at the back of the room questioned with all sincerity, "What else is there to talk about?" The teacher remembered that inquiry some fifty years later.

The story is relevant. Those are among the topics on which I dwell every time my hull hits water. Is it not astounding that the very concept of map making was not developed until the days of Columbus? It took several hundred years later to create longitude. Anyone who has had the audacity or stupidity to sail around the world has my greatest respect. But think about Cook or Columbus who sailed without a GPS, satellite telephone, or a laptop. Thinking about those types of people and their accomplishments are worthy of a good day aboard the boat.

THIRTY-THREE

GREY'S BOAT

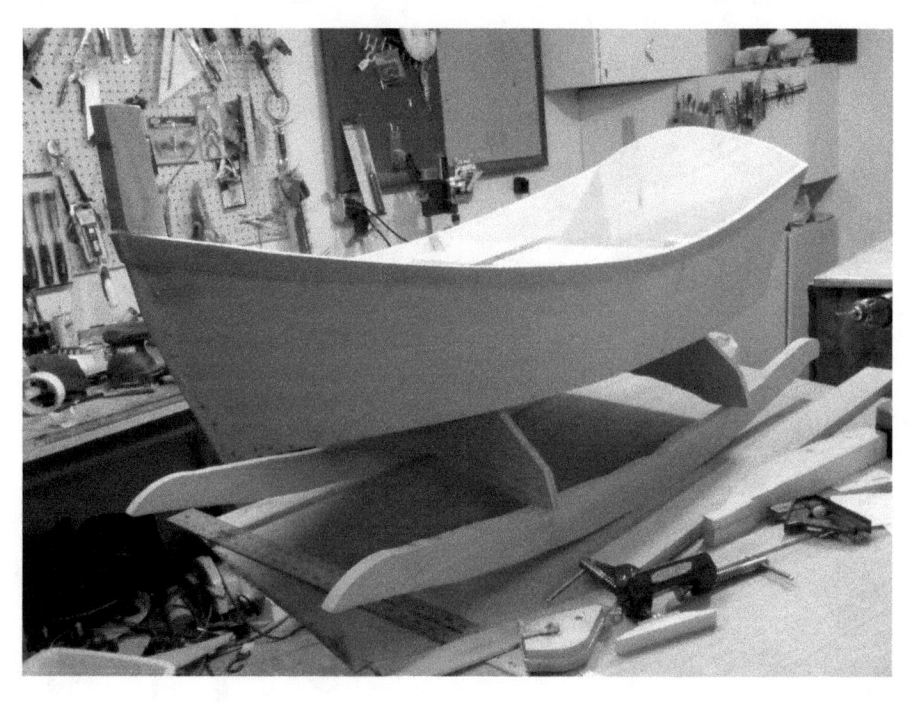

Finally, at the ripe old age of 64, I became a grandparent, a long-awaited position for which I believe I am the perfectly oriented. My doctoral dissertation was *Grandparental Influences on Locus of Control*, a somewhat lame research paper devoted to a plethora of graphs, charts, analyses of variance, correlations, Scheffe analysis of individual variables, and a modest smattering of prose written in the passive voice as per expectations for scholarly discourse. In the end, the entire project was greatly confounded by family size and gender; however, I became totally convinced that grandparents have a moral, ethical, and psychological obligation to spoil their grandchildren rotten. I have waited and waited for this opportunity.

My own grandfather, a dentist who lived just down the block, introduced me to boats. Many a day was spent on the Mississippi drowning worms, munching on crackers and summer sausage, and drinking Nehi Strawberry pop. He was the perfect grandfather and felt that mandate to spoil his grandchildren, namely my brother and me.

With this virtually religious tenet I commenced my commitment to delighting my beautiful granddaughter in all ways possible. Since I have this afflicting addiction to boats, I felt a need to build my beloved Grey Nassaria Regan a Jolly Boat Rocker as advertised in one of the surge of magazines I receive monthly. The ad clearly stated that this rocker was perfect for small children, easily constructed, and modest in cost. Even a beginner could build this boat-shaped rocker in less than three days, so said the fine print.

What I received was an envelope of 4 pages: 2 large pages with patterns and two pages of materials required to assemble this easy-to-build plus a single paragraph of simple directions. Ace Hardware and Home Depot met all my needs: several pieces of marine grade plywood, a Dewalt electric sander, ball peen hammer, saber saw, carbon paper (OK, that was picked up at Staples), and a used band saw. Unfortunately, I had to order some silicon-bronze 3/4" ring nails from West Marine. This was in January. Three days said the ad.

My first clue should have been the 3/4' silicone bronze ring nails that were $10.95 per one hundred plus $9.95 shipping and handling. They came in a small box the size of a small aspirin bottle. These were attracted to the floor of my basement where they were spilled in mass and approximately half were salvaged. It was almost February.

The pattern was transcribed via carbon paper and metal ruler to the surface of the plywood. I was so proud of myself. My little workbench is about 3'x4' and I had no cause to believe it was insufficient for my nautical creation. I started to gently cut the plywood when I found that this somewhat expensive wood material tended to splinter terribly.

Let me take a little bird walk. When I was in high school during the early 60's, intelligent and college-bound students were not allowed to enroll in certain classes such as typing (that was for future secretaries), agricultural, or Industrial Arts. We were being siphoned into physics, higher-level mathematics, chemistry, and foreign languages (Latin was important). I have, therefore, never built a birdhouse, sawn a board, drilled a hole, glued joints, or even knew what a planer was. I was busy conjugating Latin verbs, solving quadratic equations, memorizing Newton's laws, and mixing substances to obtain purple precipitates.

Interestingly, since college I have never stumbled onto a quadratic equation, was required to conjugate some Latin verb, to say nothing of making precipitates. Worse, Newton's Law's ended up in the bonfire of quantum mechanics. Sawing, drilling, and gluing have become a routine demand of a homeowner. But those skills were left to the dolts while we geniuses were supposed to fly rocket ships to Mars, solve the time-space conundrum, and develop engineering marvels. I blame it on the nuns.

Let me back up. I went to the Big Box for some plywood. It put it on my trailer that has been sitting quietly in my backyard since we moved ten years ago. Miss Frozen Finland, aka my wife, has complained that it needs to be sold but I remind her that someday we may need it. Thus, after sitting for ten years it was finally used. Driving back home I looked in my rear-view mirror to see a 4x8 sheet flying away down the road. I did not realize that plywood could fly in that fashion but fly it did. Fortunately, no one was near the street so it did not hit anything but it did shatter. Yet another lesson learned.

After securing another piece of plywood and a bunch of hardwood boards, I stenciled the pieces carefully onto the wood. Clearly any idiot could cut along the lines. Or so I thought. I cut off the excess to get down to the bare hunks to saw with immense precision; however, one brief lapse cut a section in half but with Elmer's and a little support it worked out.

Now band saws are utilized to shape curves and do intricate little minute stuff. My deluxe used model couldn't cut along a line without wobbling along like the path of a drunken sailor. Obviously, it needed adjustment. I adjusted it. I then proceeded to: a) break the band; b) break the "tire" or little rubber circle that goes around the wheel. No problem, it is a Craftsman and Sears is only 10 minutes away.

They don't make that model anymore and they had to order the stuff directly from some manufacturer in China or Viet Nam or somewhere. They were sure they could get the parts within 6 to 8 weeks.

Using my time efficiently I tried to hand cut several parts with my little old saber saw that burned out quickly. Sears sold me a new one. It worked wonderfully cutting right through the cord on my Dremel with ease. I did not know that there were blades for different types of wood. My "let's cut down sequoias" blade splintered plywood. Sears sold me appropriate blades. The new blades were wonderful as they went through the wire to my table saw that was being used as a woodworking bench.

By April I had most of the puzzle parts cut out; but some were not quite the same size or shape due to my sawing abilities (or inabilities). This required correction by significant sanding. My Dewalt electric sander of high quality and a ton of various courses of sandpaper was great. I could sand whole forests of wood raising clouds of sawdust.

The sandpaper was held to the power sander by two little wires that hooked under a plastic knob. The plastic knobs broke off quickly. Dewalt said "tough toenails".

I don't have a doctorate for nothing. I can think. I can analyze. I can create. Double-sided tape holds sandpaper much better than wires and plastic knobs. Black and Decker can bite me. Actually, when my Black and Decker drill died after less than a year of service, I tried to send it in for repair. It seems that B&D is mostly a licensing company that sells the rights for their logo and name but they do not actually manufacture, distribute, or deal with products bearing their name. Bacchus owns car products using the Black and Decker name. Others make B&D saws; a different company makes tools, etc. Harbor Freight, here I come.

The plans call for the use of 3/4 inch bronze ring nails. West Marine supplies them for a modest fee and a whooping shipping and handling fee. $10 for 100 nails! The plans say that is more than enough. Wrong, I needed another 100. I have $40 in nails which bend easily, split plywood wonderfully, and are tiny enough to get lost on my work bench/table saw. Once I was hard up for nails so I emptied the vacuum cleaner to obtain a dozen or so.

Sanding is a torturous endeavor created by maniacal nuns demanding penance for some long-forgotten set of sins, or so I believe. Nevertheless, this is incredibly boring mandating several types of sandpaper, holders, and tools. The Dewalt power sander died violently with a crack, a bang, a spark, and ball bearings shooting across the floor like zany animals that had been sniffing glue.

It is now October and the little girl's first birthday is coming up real soon. Panic has firmly ensconced itself in my feeble mind and total paralysis has gripped me. I look at the half-finished boat and am instantly seized by insatiable thirst for beer (Brandy Old Fashions are acceptable too). After enough fluid ingestion I lose the tyrant paralysis, gain some momentum, and realize that I need to work on that project, tomorrow.

Grey is standing by herself, making her initial two-legged saunter, and uttering her first words. "Grandpa" is not in her vocabulary, nor is the word "boat". She says "Joe", which is the dog's name. She cries at the sight of me and detests water. Her name is in the Last Will and Testament in pencil. Can I finish the boat in a week? How can I haul that, my wife's extensive luggage, mom and her "stuff" and the dog to St. Paul? The anguished cry you hear around the world is just this old Salt in his workroom.

Three days! Inexpensive! Easy to build! Bite my transom.

THIRTY-FOUR

ENVIRONMENT

Someone said that humans are the only ones who crap in their own nest. My wife will state differently as she cleans the zebra finch's cage. The point is depressingly clear, we are rapidly destroying our planet. Data spew forth like an erupting volcano; but political entities and Big Business ignore it in toto. I have been writing about my concerns for many years, and I get more and more frustrated.

When oil became a geopolitical issue, fracking seemed the easy solution; however, fracking needed a special kind of limestone sand to work effectively and efficiently, and America had lots of it. Unfortunately, fracking led to a plethora of problems ranging from causing earth quakes in Oklahoma to destroying roads in rural areas when big trucks inundated them carrying sand.

And then Big Business stuck its hoary fingers into the pie. In tiny White Hall, WI fracking company Hi-Crush granted their executives over $3 million in bonuses five days before declaring bankruptcy. It, unfortunately, is a snowflake example of the Alps.

A beautiful and pristine trout stream Bloody Run Creek, untouched for eons, became the focal point of the war between farmers and environmentalists near my hometown. The Walz family proposed to build a herd of 11,600 beef cattle on their farm up stream. Can you imagine the manure pile? What about the smell?

They claimed a digestor would take care of it; however, a similar operation with 1,000 cows has three times failed and allowed sewage to enter the environment. The concerns of the environmentalists are real.

The late Tim Mason, a staunch environmentalist and occasional Park Ranger at Effigy Mounds National Park, fought bravely against anything that would damage the park, Bloody Run, or Yellow River that flows past the park. His research overwhelmingly noted the uniqueness of the Driftless Zone exemplified by this area.

The Dead Zone, an area the size of Connecticut, at the mouth of the Mississippi is so poisonous that no fish or plant can survive. The deadly chemicals come from farm runoff and are composed of fertilizers, herbicides, insecticides, and fungicides. Studies indicate that Iowa is the primary concern and that up to 30% of the crud comes from Iowa. Worse, Iowa's once black, rich topsoil is now residing in Louisiana. Iowa State University studies indicate that 7-9 inches of the state's topsoil has eroded into the Missouri and Mississippi rivers.

Carbon, the primary element for all life, is also the problem in sustaining life. While this diametrically opposite concept is bewildering, it is fact. Carbon, in the form of CO_2 is killing us softly. Plants and the ocean absorb CO_2 and proffers necessary O_2 in return. This is how Mother Nature maintains homeostasis or balance. The rapid loss of forestation, especially in South America and Africa, has thrown that balance into a tizzy. The cause of deforestation is and has been for 50 years the result of overpopulation. Worse, China and India alone make up 25% of the world's inhabitants.

Industrial emissions alone warrant finger pointing. While many factories have followed the environmental protection laws, most states thumb their noses at the EPA who has little power to enforce mandates. Trucks pump approximately 154.2 tons per million ton-miles, according to a Texas Transportation Institute report. Interestingly, tugboats proffer only 15.6.

According to the US Energy Information Administration, the world pumps about 33,621 million tons of CO_2 into the air annually. The U.S. alone is responsible for 5,130 million metric tons of carbon dioxide. Most of this comes from transportation. This has quadrupled in the last 20 years. Scientists claim that within 24 years we will have enough carbon dioxide to warm the planet by a minimum of 2 degrees, a point where life as we know it will disappear as sea levels rise, polar icecaps melt, and most marine life vanishes. But who's counting?

Another major problem facing our oceans is plastic. Many circumnavigators have stated that there wasn't a single day they were afloat that they did not see waste plastic floating around. Everyone attracted to the seas is familiar with the Great Pacific Garbage Patch, an area that currents spiral around and not letting anything leave. It is twice the size of Texas at 617,000 square miles of junk. Worse, it has four cousins in the North Atlantic, South Pacific, Indian Ocean, and South Atlantic. Experts predict that within 30 years there will be more plastic in the ocean than fish.

Plastic is a generic term for hundreds of complicated chemical compounds such as polycarbonates, polyethylene, polypropylenes, polyvinyl chlorides, and even polyesters. The plastic water bottle is significantly different than the milk jug that is entirely different than the fishnets. You cannot simply collect all that stuff, melt it down, and make new stuff. It all has to be separated according to its compound-type.

Too much carbon causes acidification of the water that, in turn, results in less calcium carbonate that is necessary for shellfish and coral. 25% of all marine life depends on coral. 2 of every 3 breaths we take come from the ocean's ecology.

The Save-the-Whales campaign has been a success. The humpback population was down to 450 but now is estimated at 25,000. Other species of whale have shown increases. Whales are an essential component of our ecology and the life of oceans. Whale poop is not huge chunks, as one might expect, but little pieces that float to the surface creating an upward current bringing life-sustaining nutrients from the bottom to the surface where plankton eat it and, in turn, is eaten by fish that are eventually eaten by bigger fish down the food chain. The simply upward current itself is necessary for deep sea oxygen to be let into the air.

As a grandparent, I would hope that my little girls will not have to attempt drastic, life-altering ameliorations in order to survive. They should be able to enjoy the waters of Minnesota, kayak and canoe to their hearts content, fish for Northern pike and pan fish, not worry about what they drink from the faucet, or the air they breathe. We have messed up our globe terribly, and the planet is seeking balance. The earth is a perfect environment, except for humans. Will Mother Nature try to eradicate her biggest threat? Remember that old commercial: "Pay now or pay me later."? We are going to pay. Big time.

THIRTY-FIVE

BUYING THAT SMALL OLD BOAT

You have the fever. Oh, most definitely you have the fever to buy an old boat and fix it up because you suddenly have this dream to sail the deep blue, spend lengthy weekends on the lake, thrive in Caribbean sun while it snows in Minnesota, or some similar sudden intention. This particular contagion strikes immediately upon exposure to a boat, a dinghy, or a weekend near a harbor, or the awareness of used boats for sale. My psychological surrender came on a Mega 30 in the Apostle Islands.

While I made my initial purchase on sound principles, my second boat was made on the spur of the moment after seeing an ad on the Internet when I saw the small boat of my dreams complete with a picture and at a price I could afford. The purchase was made sight unseen.

After long and arduous contemplation of my newly beloved boat and discussion with wiser minds than mine, I commenced cogitation of what I should do in the future. While the following ideas are neither complete nor new, they do offer some meager suggestions when the fever hits.

LOOK BEFORE YOU LEAP

Long before you jump into anything like purchasing a boat, discuss it with your significant other. This may lead to disingenuous plotting but it may prevent a sudden awareness that your partner is easily seasick, is frightened of water, cannot swim, or some other rationale that makes the project boat a questionable idea. More than one sailor discovered that his dream boat and his wife were intolerable of each other.

Think about costs. Good old boats always need something and that something invariably costs a bundle. Year-to-year maintenance is not especially cheap even though you are doing the work yourself. The Do-It-Yourself boat owner will end up buying tools he or she never dreamed of. West Marine, Hamilton, Fisheries Supply and other catalogs will become weekly reading. Other costs annually may include winter storage, marina and docking fees, maybe a trailer, or out-hauling and placing on blocks.

KNOW WHAT YOU NEED

Long before you start drooling over some boat sitting forlorn at the dock just begging for tender loving care and devoted attention, know what you want and what you need. A working Iowan four hours from a major lake might want to reconsider the dream of a 62' luxury blue water boat. One friend had a boat eight hours from his home. A weekend cruise was simply out of the question. It took a long day of driving to the boat, stocking supplies, checking rigging, and general preparation. One day of sailing and then doing the reverse was beyond stamina. A four-day outing was the minimal requirement. Being able to sail only two or three times a year ended up being too little for the time and costs. Reluctantly, the owner sold his prize. Maybe a smaller, towable boat would have met his needs better.

If you are going to be doing a lot of solo sailing, a big boat probably is not the right boat; on the other hand, if you have six older children a dinghy is inappropriate. A lot of soloing in a small lake will warrant one type of boat while Great Lakes sailing with friends or a stable crew will necessitate another.

BUYING THE GOOD OLD BOAT

Coupled with knowing what you need is the actual purchasing of the boat. Before you start discussions with the bank, do lots of comparison checks. Each and every sailboat has important problems as well as inherent positives. Magazine such as SMALL BOAT ADVISOR, GOOD OLD BOAT, SAIL, MESSING AROUND IN BOATS, LATITUDES and ATTITUDES, WOODEN BOAT, and others have monthly highlights on many brands of boats. Some are built for comfort, some for speed, some for easy sailing in quiet lakes, and others for oceanic voyages in heavy seas. No boat is perfect in all aspects. If you are tall, you need headroom. If you less than nimble, you need more beam. A recent magazine review raved about a certain boat, but one had to go over the traveler to enter the cabin. Not a boat for the clumsy.

An examination by an accomplished surveyor is absolutely essential for even a small boat. Note that I did not do that when I purchased my good old boat (built in 1984) but I was lucky. The cost of a survey is well worth every penny. You will know exactly what needs to be done, what can wait, what can be ignored, or the satisfaction of knowing your boat is in perfect shape.

Search the Internet. "Yahoo Groups" has dozens of boating organizations with members more than willing to assist you. These people will give you more information than you can imagine. The positive and negative elements of each brand and model will be comprehensive. Even after the purchase, you can turn to these groups for advice or knowledge on what to do and how to do it.

A good boat yard with quality personnel is a must. They can offer a myriad of insights into various boat models while also being a place you purchase materials you will need. Hang around a boatyard and talk to the people who are working on their own boats. A wealth of knowledge is lingering around behind the building. A warm Saturday is a great time to wander around, talk with people, and learn. You might also spot the perfect small craft or become apprised of one nearby.

Asking lots of questions is legitimate and, surprisingly, most sailors truly enjoy assisting others. Discovering a boating guru is a delight. My personal friend, fellow sailor, and boat builder is a former Coast Guard seaman and lockmaster, (Mississippi Bob) who is on my phone's speed dial. He can answer virtually all my questions or can tell me whom to call. Just hanging around him is an education unto itself. Find yourself a similar guardian angel.

DON'T GO BEYOND SKILLS

Many boats look like easy fixes. While a challenge is always fun, getting in over your head can be painful and expensive.

For the small boat crowd, this means don't buy a boat that requires working skills with which you are not familiar. A boat that requires significant fiberglass repair, engine overhauling, and internal electrical work might be incredibly expensive or demand more than you have the time and experience to do yourself. Of course, this does not mean to say you cannot learn these skills. On the contrary, a first-time boat buyer will discover a whole new realm of skills that will be developed. For many people, just fooling around on the boat making little repairs, varnishing, polishing, cleaning, reworking, painting, and the like will be as rewarding as the sailing itself. If you have a good old boat, you better develop this attitude because the older the boat, the more work is required. If you are time-strapped, then an older boat is not for you. If you don't know a hack saw from a screwdriver, take a class or learn from somebody who will take you under wing. Still, keep your repairs within your skill level.

LEARN FROM MISTAKES

You will make about hundreds of mistakes. Get used to it. Learn from them. Do not be afraid to ask lots of questions about what should have done correctly. Making correct decisions come from experience, and experience comes from making mistakes. Small boat sailors are a wonderful bunch and will offer suggestions and advice, usually based on lessons they learned from doing the same thing. Admitting that we have made foolish errors is a most difficult task but it is not the mistake that is important, it is the lesson learned. Personally, I hate experiential learning because I have to make the goof twice before I fully understand a better solution. Nevertheless, the more mistakes we make, the more we learn. In time, newbie sailors will face similar situations and knew exactly what to do.

A good logbook can be anything from a cheap spiral notebook to some sort of monogrammed leather covered and homemade-paper bound journal. The key is to note weather conditions, wind speed, temperature, but most of all it should contain anecdotal accounts of issues, problems, solutions or ideas for the future. Periodic review of your log will offer ideas for replacement or repair needs, advice on future responses to problems, and reminders of what you need to do.

The log is a superb way to spend the non-sailing season reviewing your learning from the previous summer. If you carefully include items that are nonessential but on a To-Do list for later action, you will find a wonderful reminder of how you can spend the off months improving your good old boat. For example, this winter I have to clean the sails, wash the lines, repair the main sail, fix a loose cleat, drill a hole in my center board for better holding power in the upright position. My log also reminds me that there is some basic hull painting that needs to be done early in the spring, and that the boat needs to be re-licensed in April.

SUBSCRIBE

This article is not intended to be the Be All/End All for people about to enter the world of the good old boats; however, it is a beginning. The one thing that all good sailors need to do can be summed up in three words: subscribe, subscribe, and subscribe.

The plethora of magazines available to readers is immense but worth every penny. For small boat or trailer sailors SMALL CRAFT ADVISOR, SHALLOW WATER SAILOR and MESSING ABOUT IN BOATS are wonderful. Clearly, GOOD OLD BOAT is a must and LATTITUDES AND ATTITUDES offers information and interesting articles for cruisers. Even if you do not own a wooden boat, WOODEN BOAT prints tons of ideas from building your own furling system to working with epoxy. SAIL has good ideas for boaters in spite of its slickness and preponderancy to cater to the rich and owners of very expensive and very large boats.

Reading about fun adventures, new equipment, some easy repair proposals, and just plain entertainment warrants your subscription fee. You can learn a great deal just from magazines. Do not hesitate to write to the authors via the magazine's offices. Virtually all of them will respond with specific answers to your questions, many will follow up with additional advice, and some may well become good friends and invite you to sundry events.

While this has been a small attempt to proffer ideas for future owners of good old boats, it clearly fails to cover all the things you should be thinking about. But if you pay attention to these ideas you're purchasing and initial years of sailing in your good old boat will be fun, adventuresome, and some of the best times of your life.

THIRTY-SIX

RIPPLES IN THE WIND

An old parish priest once proffered a sermon about various concerns in life. He eloquently stated that most issues fall into two categories: irritants and problems. He said that if we dealt with the problems and ignored the irritations of life, we probably would all be much happier people. In other words, work on the problems and skip the small stuff – and most stuff is small stuff.

I failed to listen well. As a university academic dean, I once listened to my science faculty wail and gnash their teeth about the annual high school science fair that we held. In spite of the fact that I was warned that science and math professors are notorious complainers, I perceived their concerns as a major problem. I thus eliminated the science fair the next year and moved that money to another budget item.

En mass, the Fabulous Baker Boys, my nickname for them since they were all male and all taught in Baker Hall, descended upon my office with boiling blood, a lengthy rail, a bag of feathers, and a bucket of tar. How dare I end their once-a-year opportunity to show off their departments to potential students! This was a magnificent chance to be seen by teachers and students, and for the professors to recruit good science and math kids. In my feeble mind I had seen an irritation as a problem. Their complaining was all about workloads and little to do with actual problems with the science fair. Major lesson learned!

The other day the breeze was fresh, the sun was shining, and my schedule was open so I hitched up GENNY SEA to the old Subaru and headed for the lake. Upon raising the mast, I discovered the main halyard had worked loose, and I had to lower the mast with difficulty and replace the sheet. T'was more work than I wanted. Then I realized that a jib hank was broken and nothing was in my bag of tricks to make a substitute.

As I finally left the dock a full hour after arriving, I forgot to lower the center board and got blown half way to Minnesota before I realized my failure. Upon lowering the centerboard, I managed to break a block making the raising of said board damn hard work.

Nevertheless, the sun was shining, the wind was perfect, and the boat performed even with the ugly jib and its missing hank. I recovered a child's water tube and had to tack several times to reach the beach to return it. The wind was on my nose so that I could not go upstream in this man-made lake but could only go back and forth in the narrows. I stayed three hours and attained a decent sunburn. Upon arrival at the dock, I managed to kick my insulated cup overboard and reaching for it I managed to fall overboard -- cell phone and all.

When I reached home and started to enter the day's experience in my boat's log, I realized that this was nothing more than a whole batch of irritations. It was a great day of sailing.

Nay, it was damn near a perfect day..

ACKNOWLEDGEMENTS

Most of the material in this book has been published in other magazines and journals and used with permission. I am grateful to Bob Hicks, editor of the now defunct *MESSING ABOUT IN BOATS*, who not only printed my ramblings, but printed my monthly article on maritime and nautical affairs. The Naval Historical and Heritage Center kindly gave me access to the incredible records held at the Washington Navy Yard. A multitude of sailing friends offered me information and assistance along my sailing journey. The late Mississippi Bob Brown, who is missed greatly, gave me more advice than I can retain, Joe Rhomberg initiated the mania of sailing by taking me on my first sail in the Apostle Islands.

My wife, Marianne, a native of Finland, has allowed me to squander much time at the computer writing "stuff" and looking at all sorts of things nautical. I forgive her for the chronic nagging about too many sailing magazines piled on the coffee table, bedside stand, and on the floor. She has endured my teasing for 49 years. Not joyfully.

The gang at the Lake McBride sailboat storage area has been a wealth of knowledge and stories.

My beloved grandparents, Dr. Roy H. and Zonona Wheat (Feats and Nanny), started my love of reading, boating, and ethical thinking regarding nature. They set the standard.

Outskirts consultant, Tia Henshaw, warrants a special thank you for her patience.

Doc Regan is a retired educator, writer, historian, and sailor of small boats. He holds four degrees including a doctorate in educational psychology from the University of South Dakota. He was asked to return to his undergraduate college, Upper Iowa University, as Academic Dean. For a goodly portion of his career he wrote naval history. He is the biographer of Admiral Frank Jack Fletcher (*In Bitter Tempest*) and participate in the *Re-fighting World War II in the Pacific*. His writings also include articles in *Proceedings* of the U.S. Naval Institute and Naval History. His monthly article on nautical and maritime affairs was in *Messing About in Boats*. He has received several awards for his professional writing.

Doc is the former president of the Cedar Rapids Navy League and the Iowa Chapter of the Navy League. He belongs to a multitude of veteran organizations and was a director of the USS IOWA (SSN-797) Commissioning Committee.

Regan is a minion to his wife, pug, cat, and zebra finches in Cedar Rapids, IA where he sails his West Wight Potter in farm ponds, man-made lakes, and any other water that can float a boat.

CPSIA information can be obtained
at www.ICGtesting.com
Printed in the USA
BVHW032354251022
650210BV00007B/108

9 781977 258397